THE FINANCIAL MANAGER'S GUIDE TO MICROSOFTWARE

THE WILEY/RONALD-NATIONAL ASSOCIATION OF ACCOUNTANTS PROFESSIONAL BOOK SERIES

Jack Fox • ***Starting and Building Your Own Accounting Business***

Denis W. Day • ***The Corporate Guide to Business Travel Savings***

Gerald M. Ward and Jonathan D. Harris • ***Managing Computer Risks: A Guide for the Policymaker***

Harvey L. Shuster and Ray D. Dillon • ***The Financial Manager's Guide to Microsoftware***

THE FINANCIAL MANAGER'S GUIDE TO MICROSOFTWARE

HARVEY L. SHUSTER, CPA

and

RAY D. DILLON, Ph.D.

Atlanta, Georgia

WILEY

JOHN WILEY & SONS

New York • Chichester • Brisbane • Toronto • Singapore

This publication is designed to provide accurate and authoritative information in regard to the subject matter covered. It is sold with the understanding that the publisher is not engaged in rendering legal, accounting, or other professional service. If legal advice or other expert assistance is required, the services of a competent professional person should be sought. *From a Declaration of Principles jointly adopted by a Committee of the American Bar Association and a Committee of Publishers.*

Library of Congress Cataloging in Publication Data:

Shuster, Harvey L.
The financial manager's guide to microsoftware.

(The Wiley/Ronald-National Association of Accountants professional book series)
Bibliography: p.
1. Corporations—Finance—Data processing.
2. Corporations—Finance—Computer programs.
I. Dillon, Ray D. II. Title. III. Series.

HG4012.5.S47 1988 658.1'5'o285536 87-21663
ISBN 0-471-81176-9

Printed in the United States of America

10 9 8 7 6 5 4 3 2 1

This book is dedicated to the memory of
Beatrice Schildkraut

and to a future computer star:
Heather Shuster

TRADEMARK ACKNOWLEDGMENTS

THE FOLLOWING PRODUCTS ARE TRADEMARKS OF THE INDICATED COMPANIES

CLICK ART	BY	T/MAKER
dBASE III	BY	ASHTON-TATE
DECISION MAKER	BY	SOFTWARE STRATEGIES, INC.
DISPLAY WRITE III	BY	IBM
FORMULA	BY	LIFEBOAT ASSOCIATES
FRAMEWORK	BY	ASHTON-TATE
FRONT PAGE	BY	STUDIO SOFTWARE
IQ	BY	INTELLIGENT QUERY
KNOWLEDGEMAN	BY	MICRODATA BASE SYSTEMS, INC./CONS. PR.
LOTUS 1-2-3	BY	LOTUS DEVELOPMENT CORP.
1-2-3 REPORTWRITER	BY	LOTUS DEVELOPMENT CORP.
LOTUS FREELANCE	BY	LOTUS DEVELOPMENT CORP.
LOTUS GRAPHWRITER	BY	LOTUS DEVELOPMENT CORP.
LOTUS HAL	BY	LOTUS DEVELOPMENT CORP.
MS-DOS	BY	MICROSOFT CORP.
MULTIMATE	BY	MULTIMATE INTERNATIONAL CORP.
MULTIPLAN	BY	MICROSOFT CORP.
NOTE-IT	BY	TURNER HALL PUBLISHING
PAGEMAKER	BY	ALDUS
PC-DOCUMENT	BY	SYSTEMS MANAGEMENT ASSOCIATES
PC-DOS	BY	IBM
PC-WRITE	BY	QUICKSOFT

PEACHTEXT	BY	PEACHTREE SOFTWARE, INC.
PFS:WRITE	BY	SOFTWARE PUBLISHING CORP.
PFS:FILE	BY	SOFTWARE PUBLISHING CORP.
PFS:FIRST CHOICE	BY	SOFTWARE PUBLISHING CORP.
RBASE	BY	MICRORIM
SAMNA WORD	BY	SAMNA CORP.
SIDEKICK	BY	BORLAND INTERNATIONAL
SIDEWAYS	BY	FUNK SOFTWARE
SPELLBINDER	BY	LEXISOFT
SPOTLIGHT	BY	LOTUS DEVELOPMENT CORP.
SQZ!	BY	TURNER HALL PUBLISHING
SUPERCALC	BY	COMPUTER ASSOCIATES, INC.
SYMPHONY	BY	LOTUS DEVELOPMENT CORP.
THE SPREADSHEET AUDITOR	BY	CONSUMERS SOFTWARE, INC.
WHAT'S BEST	BY	GENERAL OPTIMIZATION, INC.
WORDPERFECT	BY	SATELLITE SOFTWARE INTERNATIONAL
WORDSTAR	BY	MICROPRO INTERNATIONAL CORP.

WE HAVE TRIED TO SUPPLY INFORMATION ABOUT COMPANY TRADEMARKS. TRADEMARKS INDICATED WERE DERIVED FROM VARIOUS SOURCES. HOWEVER WE CANNOT ATTEST TO THE ACCURACY OF THIS INFORMATION. OTHER PRODUCTS MENTIONED ARE ACCOMPANIED BY THEIR COMPANY NAMES AND ARE TRADEMARKS OF THOSE COMPANIES.

ACKNOWLEDGMENTS

We would like to especially thank Sheldon Hall for writing most of chapters 5, 7, 10, and 14.

Also we would like to thank Carolyn Wheeler, who reviewed and typed most of the book; Richard Millman, CPA, Partner of Seidman & Seidman; and many others.

H.L.S.
R.D.D.

CONTENTS

PART THREE TOOLS THAT HELP YOU USE MICROCOMPUTERS

THE FINANCIAL MANAGER'S GUIDE TO MICROSOFTWARE

INTRODUCTION

"Put it before them briefly so they can read it, clearly so they will appreciate it, and picturesquely so they will remember it."

Joseph Pulitzer

The *Financial Manager's Guide to Microsoftware* is designed to fulfill all of those aspects through the use of checklists, charts, overviews, outlines, and specific topic treatment. It does not concentrate on new aspects, but rather on putting the vast and confusing microsoftware world into perspective so it will be easier to know how, when, and where to apply the specific tools available. It is not the purpose of this guide to describe new, astonishing microsoftware. Based on the authors' practical experience, it puts the confusing reality into perspective.

Cost and size reductions have placed computers within the grasp of everyone from business managers to personal computer hobbyists. The increases in computing power and reliability have ensured their use in an incredible variety of applications never before feasible.

However, because developments in computer programming technology have come more rapidly than people were trained to make use of them, there is a "people gap." This involves you and me. Even the trained person has difficulty keeping up the rapid pace of hardware and software development. Professionals who have not been exposed to the technology, and yet need to be able to apply it, get left even farther behind—widening the people gap even more. In the long run the people gap will be decreased by education. The computer will be to our children's lives what the telephone and car are to the lives of our current working generation.

The purpose of this book is to be a helpful guide through the confusing and complex world of microcomputer software. It is written for treasurers, controllers, CPAs, company accountants, small company principals, top executives, and all types of financial managers. It presents guidelines in the form of tips and aids on how to:

Make use of the power of the microcomputer in a normal workday.

Gain quick access to critical information rather than wait for it to filter back (sometimes slowly, sometimes incorrectly, and sometimes not at all).

Increase individual productivity with the use of a microcomputer without extensive technical training or expertise.

To accomplish its purpose, this book:

Provides useful tools through forms, charts, and checklists.

Suggests software available for financial applications and ways to apply them more productively.

Offers ideas on how to use business software effectively through the use of examples and cases.

Shows how to avoid problems in the utilization of certain software.

Microcomputer power has not always been effectively utilized. Often only superficial use is made of the microcomputer by the executive or manager. This book guides financially-oriented individuals through the people-software gap. It is intended to assist business managers in utilizing software application for financial purposes.

This guide is intended to increase productivity through the use of basic business microsoftware products. It is not aimed at any particular package, but rather at a broad range of business software. It concentrates on the realistic utilization and limitations of the software. The basic application must be utilized effectively before it is possible to use state-of-the-art features such as windows or mouses. However, it is necessary to deal with state of the art in software technology. Microcomputer technology is an amazing field and growing rapidly. What is a mouse, a window, or a template in everyday English? It is a chore in itself to learn to speak computerese, which has become a language in itself like French or Spanish. A whole new language is being spoken by our kids and the new microcomputer experts. This language barrier increases the people gap. Before you can do anything you have to know what the computer people are talking about. This guide to microsoftware:

Explains the terminology as it goes.

Suggests books specifically on the topic of computer definitions.

Explains how to use the currently available business applications and how not to use them.

Software was first written only for computers. Today, software must be written for people as well. The reality of microsoftware is here and must be dealt with without a head-on collision. Benefits as well as limitations must be considered. It is a tool like any other technology like the telephone or car. It can substantially increase information transfer like the telephone or aid in accessibility like the car. However, a computer can kill financially as a car can physically. The computer's power is similar to the electricity that runs it. It can light the way or it can shock the user. However, the computer's power is available and it would be unfortunate if it was not harnessed for business use effectively. It can save a tremendous number of hours and provide an extensive amount of information. However, if not installed properly or applied effectively, it can cause decreases in productivity—even below the productivity levels of a manual system. The struggle between the available power and computer risks are considered in this guide.

The intent is not to discuss all software nor all approaches in dealing with the software. It is also not intended for the very sophisticated user who would do a lengthy needs analysis and mainframe type analysis in the microworld. This book is oriented more to the "quick hit" philosophy in the microworld and the instability in it.

Most companies, large and small, are trying to realize the tremendous value of the microcomputer and are scrambling to put it to use. The biggest problem they face is how best to do this and how to control the personal freedom it offers at the same time. Until very recently, the microcomputer field was the province of the hobbyists and mainframe computer technicians. The literature in the field reflects this. There is a desperate need among financial people for specific, useful information on how to use a micro in business effectively—information that is neither technical nor simple-minded.

Outstanding features of this guide:

It has a real-world approach to the use of microcomputers and the software currently available on the market. The busy executive cannot be expected to learn a programming language and is not interested in microcomputers as a hobby. Users want practical, useful service from an investment that can save time or money, preferably both.

It is intended to be specifically enlightening and especially useful through its forms and checklists. Each chapter can be a book in itself.

It provides the nontechnical financial person with an overview of the productivity possibilities and some tips for achieving improved productivity.

Who should read this book?

All business professionals who are interested in using or controlling current software technology or who need to know about it

Financial professionals who do not necessarily need to use computers however do need access to the information stored in it

Those who are responsible for utilizing microcomputers in their organization

In addition, it is written for nontechnical people as well as those knowledgeable with the technology.

The range of personnel who can use this guide:

From the top executive to the person who performs analysis for other top level executives

From the vice-president of finance, treasurer, controller to the staff accountants

From the CPA partner to the junior auditor

The guide should help you to take your computer out of the closet or to never put it in the closet.

PUTTING SOFTWARE INTO SQUARE HOLES

To help the reader deal with this whole subject, two software classifications are used in this book:

Office productivity

Accounting

These categories are used because it is necessary to have some logical structure to understand microsoftware. This structure is shown in Chapter 1, Figure 1–3.

Office Productivity

Solutions or tools to apply to individual tasks not related to specific accounting or record-keeping functions.

Office productivity software includes electronic spreadsheets, word processing, and communications tools.

These increase productivity through user-definable tasks for a specific functional area:

Calculating

Writing

Talking

Drawing

Planning

Since their introduction, electronic spreadsheets have been adored by financial people. Their ability to increase productivity by calculating, recalculating, and reporting the results of analysis projects is phenomenal.

Other tools that offer great capabilities are graphics, word processing, and project management.

These tools allow for sophisticated microcomputer usage. Previously, on larger computers, many of these applications were not feasible or were too cumbersome. An example is the large company that continued doing budgeting on the mainframe instead of the microcomputer:

On the Mainframe *Two-day Event*	*On the Microcomputer* *Minutes Required*
1. Enter information into a package that creates a spreadsheet (software that is entered by line creates a spreadsheet).	1. Enter information into electronic spreadsheet. Calculations done automatically.

2. Wait for spreadsheet to be processed.	2. Redo and print report right in the software.
3. Redo if changes are needed.	3. Get report the same day, within minutes after entering.
4. Wait in line for report to print.	4. Print graph immediately.
5. Pick up report next day in the data processing department.	5. Telecommunicate, if desired, to another person.
	All steps are performed by the user without waiting.

In a combination of technologies, microcomputers will just fold into the world as a powerful tool by using:

Telecommunications
Mainframe—microlinks
Mini—microlinks
External data bases
Multiuser systems
Networking
Telephone, computer hookups

Within the office productivity world

Data base management systems (DBMS)

Create files in a systematic manner with flexible file building software.
Can create tailored record-keeping applications
Sort data in a predefined or in a redefined manner
Maintain information stored in a previously established file structure

There are three basic types of data base managers:

List managers
Simple DBMS (frequently included as one part of integrated office productivity software)
Extensive or sophisticated DBMS

List managers and data base managers are classified as office productivity tools, although they can be used as an accounting tool, as can the electronic spreadsheet. They are sometimes combined and sold with electronic spreadsheets and word processors. A data base manager is included in Symphony[tm], a product of Lotus Development Corporation, and is an integral part of the word processing, electronic spreadsheet, and graphic capacities, working in conjunction with them. List managers and data base managers are just simpler versions of the extensive DBMS products that are available, such as dBaseIII[tm], Formula[tm], and RBase[tm].

The extensive or more sophisticated data base managers provide much more flexibility, creating a programming-type language capability. These products allow many diverse functions to be performed, rather than a specific application such as doing a receivable function. List managers can list customers and inventory items. Data base managers can perform many other functions. They are powerful tools that can be applied to many clerical, analysis, or record-keeping functions.

Accounting

Computerizes the manual accounting functions

Does general bookkeeping

Processes customer orders

Sends out bills and statements to customers

Pays employees

Pays bills

Maintains and records perpetual inventories

Because of the size of the information being handled even in small businesses, manual record-keeping can be tedious, time-consuming, and uninformative on a timely basis.

Consider the accounts receivable function alone. How easy is it in many companies to obtain an accounts receivable aging? On a micro you just go to the correct menu, press a few keys, and you have the report weekly, compared to manual systems where you get them monthly, if at all. With this information, cash flow can be improved. In inventory, information control and speed can be enormous compared with a manual system of perpetual cards—one for each inventory item. Imagine the reporting ability of a computerized inventory system compared to the process of reviewing and writing down similar information based on a stack of cards. For example, from the *Quick* computer reports you can obtain:

Current stocking levels

Lists to take a physical inventory

Categorization of inventory by various methods

Turnover information

Economic order quantities

Reporting is not the only benefit. Just storing and manipulating the numbers is significant in itself. Typing and updating automatically perpetual inventory computer files is much faster than finding the right perpetual inventory card, posting the number, and then adding or subtracting it.

The world is not flat! The world is round, as is the microsoftware world. Nice neat boxes for categorizing software may not work all the time. The integration of software combines the individual capability of one specific product to another. Here one plus one can equal three. Products such as Symphony[tm], Framework[tm], Decisionmaker[tm], and RBase[tm] combine office productivity with a data base manager to create greater power than the individual pieces. They are not as easy to group as an electronic spreadsheet, therefore learning and applying them takes longer. In addition, accounting software added to word processing or electronic spreadsheets is another integration that provides for one plus one equals three. Many accounting packages are being written with data base managers as their foundation and integrated to office productivity tools to complete the circle.

Do not try to overapply or overbuy. A small success is far better than a large failure. All of these tools can be utilized in a staged approach.

New microsoftware is being released at a rapid rate. Many represent new capabilities of existing products; some represent totally new concepts; some have no substance or worth. They should be understood before assuming they are required. Just as with some of the currently available software, there will be new applications and uses that are counterproductive. They will create new countries in the microsoftware world and new worlds within themselves, especially considering handwritten computer input, voice recognition, and artificial intelligence.

DON'T READ THIS BOOK! USE IT AS A REFERENCE!

This book was not written to be read from cover to cover. It will not teach you how to program in BASIC, nor will it give you definitions or a generalized view of what microcomputers are. What it will do is:

Provide insight into specific types of software.

Give specific suggestions on how to increase your microcomputer knowledge.

Offer suggestions on how you can use a microcomputer to increase productivity.

Provide real world applications for the types of software discussed in the book.

Supply checklists, charts, and examples of how to use the applications discussed.

It is not a book about specific packages. For example, the comments on electronic spreadsheets could apply to almost any spreadsheet package that functions with rows and columns as its basis.

Although this book is not technically bound to any one type of computer or specific software product, it does include examples of specific products that are available in the market today and that the reader could expect to be interested in buying. There are checklists included to show the relative usefulness of different products, and basic forms to help the reader set up practical aids and applications. This guide shows the financial manager how to set up a financial statement analysis using a spreadsheet package. The approach used in the book is intended to accommodate the leading products in the financial field.

This book is organized as a structured reference approach to micro-software for business. There are three independent parts:

PART I The World of Microcomputer Software

PART II Software That Counts

PART III Tools That Help You Use Microcomputers

These parts are organized as follows:

PART I

A. Overview of the microcomputer system

B. A look through the microsoftware world

PART II

A. Two major classifications for business microsoftware: office productivity and accounting

B. Representative software applications within each general category

C. Approaches to applying these packages more productively

D. Features in these packages that can reduce their usefulness

E. Popular software packages in each classification

To review a specific type of software, refer to the chapter that covers it.

PART III

A. Charts, checklists, and lists that aid in the knowledge and productive use of micros in business applications

B. Explanation of concepts that facilitate use of commands and functions in software, such as designing your own reference cards

C. Keyboard overlays and templates that maintain certain preestablished routine functions that you specifically perform

D. Steps for protection of software data

E. Lists for reference material, whether magazines, newsletters, or books to sustain updated knowledge

F. A wide range of useful information that aids in dealing productively with the microcomputer world

PART ONE

THE WORLD OF MICROCOMPUTER SOFTWARE

1

A HISTORICAL PERSPECTIVE

WHAT WAS, WHAT IS, WHAT WILL BE

The first sound from a wire—when Bell said, "Mr. Watson, come here. I want you!"—set a new course for all of us. The first computer, ENIAC, in the 1940s and the microcomputer today are a part of this evolving technology. Microcomputers are a part of the greater informational and technological revolution as shown in the following chart. As history is demonstrating, the microcomputer—once considered a toy—is becoming an integral part of society in the handling and transfering of information.

The following provides a historical perspective and explains where microcomputers fit into the dramatic technological change of the late 19th and 20th centuries. It is part of the evolving technology being passed down to the individual.

Technological Evolution to Microcomputer and Beyond: Late Nineteenth Century and the Twentieth Century

1870s	Telephone	Bell
	Lightbulb	With filament of carbonized thread
1900s	Automobile	Mass produced in the United States
	Vacuum tube	
1910s	Talking pictures	Edison

1930s	Television	Regular broadcasts in the United States
1940s	Computer	ENIAC computer, transistors
1950s	UNIVAC	Mass produced, commercially available computer
1970s	Microprocessor	
Mid-1970s	Microcomputers commercially available—release of APPLE and standardized microsoftware	
1981	IBM's release of business microcomputer	
Early 1980s	Microcomputers released by almost every major computer hardware manufacturer	

In the 1980s, cumulative technological advances have already resulted in:

1. Integrating technology
   Micro to minicomputers and mainframe
   Office productivity to accounting to data bases
2. Connecting all electronic devices—micros, creating networks of technological equipment—telephone networks and computers.
3. Handwritten computer input recognition
4. Voice recognition advances
5. Advances in artificial intelligence

By 2001, total artificial intelligence (The movie *2001: A Space Odyssey* demonstrated the power of a futuristic computer)	Intelligent and voice communicative computer

We are at the beginning of the computer's evolution. The microcomputer, once thought of as a stand-alone machine, has great power through its connection to the world as well as its own internal operational abilities.

The microcomputer is in its infancy because commercial business microcomputers were only first seen in 1975. Then, in 1981, IBM provided legitimacy to the micro for business use. Obviously, the microcomputer is a new tool with little history to aid in determining what is right and what is wrong. In addition, the significantly changing power of this tool increases the lack of knowledge.

Previously, computers were touched only by trained data processing professionals. With the micro, the computer is available to every financial professional as a integral business tool. Before, only structured use took place. Now, these little machines can appear anywhere. Their greater power is available to everyone who wants to use it. The people gap must be filled to use new software applications that take advantage of the new, larger, and faster microcomputers—mainframe capacity on an individual's desk. The people gap must be filled because the software gap between hardware and software technology is beginning to close.

You need to know:

What the computer is

What it is not

What it can do

What it cannot do

What it should do

What it should not do

We cannot all be swept away by the excitement and the high technology fever. If we are, then microcomputers will continue to end up in closets when they cannot be effectively applied. The old cost-benefit analysis will win in the long run. It will determine if, when, and where microcomputers should be applied. Controlling, planning, and using effective methods in applying microcomputers are necessary. The micro revolution was intended to put in all of our hands the power of the computer and provide for technological freedom.

Many times micros are purchased under the manager's own authority; they are inexpensive enough so that the approval of the Manager of Information Systems (MIS) is not required. The individual manager wants to use computer power and have computer freedom. However, this does not ensure integrity of data and control by the total organization.

A precarious balance has to be created between individual technology freedoms and control to assure productivity and consistency with the company's total system.

WHERE'S SOFTWARE?

Software is the key to the microcomputer's power. It drives the computer through preestablished instructions with input by the operator. The hardware is the physical component; the software is the interacting producer of the user's desires.

The software referred to in this book is standard or packaged software—that is, software produced to be sold to many users in general, and not customized for an individual computer user. The revolutionary concept in the industrial revolution and the auto industry was the production line, the ability to mass produce a product. With the quantities of software now being produced, standard software has achieved its concept of being mass produced for general consumption. Due to the low pricing of micros, the pressure to create standard software is even greater.

Software is the instructions that tell the computer what to do. If actually seen or listed, it is lines of letters, numbers, symbols, and words or code that is in the format of a specific computer language like BASIC or COBOL.

Even so, "the software is the key" reality is being fought by the computer manufacturers and retail stores. The profit margins are in the hardware. Software frequently is a means to move the computer. You, the user, must make this choice. Select the software first in a purchase decision. Spend time on deciding the type of application needed and applying it most productively.

The following market factors affect what is available:

1. The reduction in microcomputer pricing is occurring while the cost of software relative to the hardware stays up.
2. The base technology on a single user system is changing slower than developments in software.
3. The advent of the multiuser micro is applying price pressure on the single user hardware.
4. The same price pressure does not exist on the software.
5. The immediate gratification from microcomputers wanes with concern for the right matching of:

Software

Computers

Terminals

Telecommunication devices

Greater application has been given to evaluating the software as the key to the productive use of the microcomputer's power.

New generations of software are being announced. Previously, software was developed to suit the limitations of computers. In the future, software will be written to suit people. This change is also affecting current software.

Most accounting micro applications are a computerization of the way bookkeeping is done manually. They do not take advantage of the microcomputer technology. In the future this should change.

The first releases of microsoftware were just computer codes, the instructions on a diskette. Later, people who had to use the program and could not talk to the developer required written instructions on paper—hence documentation. The current round includes training and support. Four major components of business microsoftware are:

I. Program on a diskette
II. Documentation
III. Aids in software utilization
 A. Training aids
  1. Tutorials
  2. Computer-aided training
  3. Training classes
 B. Reference cards
IV. Support and Policies

These components are discussed in detail in Table 1–1.

The importance of each one depends on the application and the user's level of knowledge. Each component should be weighted accordingly for each application.

Training allows the user to quickly apply the application to a specific use. The people gap is being filled by:

Training centers

Tutorials

Table 1–1. Example of Items to Look for in Software

Part of Software Package	What it is	What to look for
I. Software Programs	Instructions to computer normally delivered on diskette	Program has source code delivered with it or available so program can be modified by user and also supported by user, if necessary
		Program written in standard computer languages: BASIC, COBOL, RPG, and so forth
		Program written in structured fashion
		Program portable to a number of types of computers
		Program was or will be upgraded
		Files can be interfaced with other software and have the ability to be communicated
		Menu driven with submenu structure
		Program has ability to get to submenu functions without going back to the main menu
		Program edits fields: alphanumeric or numeric
		Is it easy to read?
		Complete and easy to read manual shows all screens that will appear in system and all reports generated by system.
II. Documentation	Instructions to the user on how to use the software and what it does	What determines a valid account number?
	Normally delivered in a binder or on diskette	
	Reference material for operations	

TABLE 1–1. Continued

Part of Software Package	What it is	What to look for
		What are the security features? What is the number of characters that are valid in an entry? Does each report have to be run before the next one can be requested? How is the manual organized? Are there tabbed sections for each task? Installation Daily processing or commands Reporting options Is there clarity and conciousness of the documentation? Is it indexed and cross-referenced? Is it accurate? Does it explain all functions in enough detail? Do you know what security features are available? Does it explain all controls in system (such as the passwords)? Does it give you the error messages and telephone number for support?
III. Aids in software utilization	Any items outside of the basic programs and reference documentation that assist the user in: Learning Installing Operating Creating more Productive use	Training Materials: In separate binders Computer-based training Self-instructional Practice sets and exercises Sample data included in software to use for practice

TABLE 1–1. Continued

Part of Software Package	What it is	What to look for
		Reference card—separate card to be placed near the computer for daily use. Found frequently with office productivity software. May include: List of commands Index of functions Critical operating information and instructions Reminder of codes Index and reference to manual Keyboard overlays—for software that uses specific keys on the keyboard to perform specific functions like EDIT or HELP facility. Plastic overlay fits over keys indicating what they do Show functions of specific keys Specific instructions concerning the keys Help facility—on diskette with program Provides help in performing a function or describes specific operation of software Assists at a specific point in the program with information about an entry such as the letters allowed
IV. Support and policies	Includes extra help the software vendor can provide and the policies of vendors	Training classes Updates for programs (especially useful for payroll and tax prepartion packages)

TABLE 1–1. Continued

Part of Software Package	What it is	What to look for
		Telephone support from the software vendor Number of telephone lines vendor has and response time Operational problems explained and solved Program problems explained and solved Is there a site license (software allowed to be installed on more than one computer in an organization based on one license)? Update policies Trial period

Computer-based training (interactive video disk training)

Quick reference materials such as reference cards

Documentation on the diskette

A user may have only four hours to grasp the use of a piece of software and apply it to a specific situation. Reading extensive manuals for many products can be very difficult. Tools such as those discussed in Part III can help. To create productive uses quickly, greater emphasis on this problem is needed. One user can grasp only so many packages with so many different command structures.

Software should be viewed as a tool. If you use a calculator for mathematical computations, then use an electronic spreadsheet for larger recurring computations or analysis.

1. Preview the software.
2. Make your selection.
3. Use the software like any other electronic tool.

You know you are going to make calls, so you purchase a phone. If you prepare financial analyses that suit a spreadsheet, then:

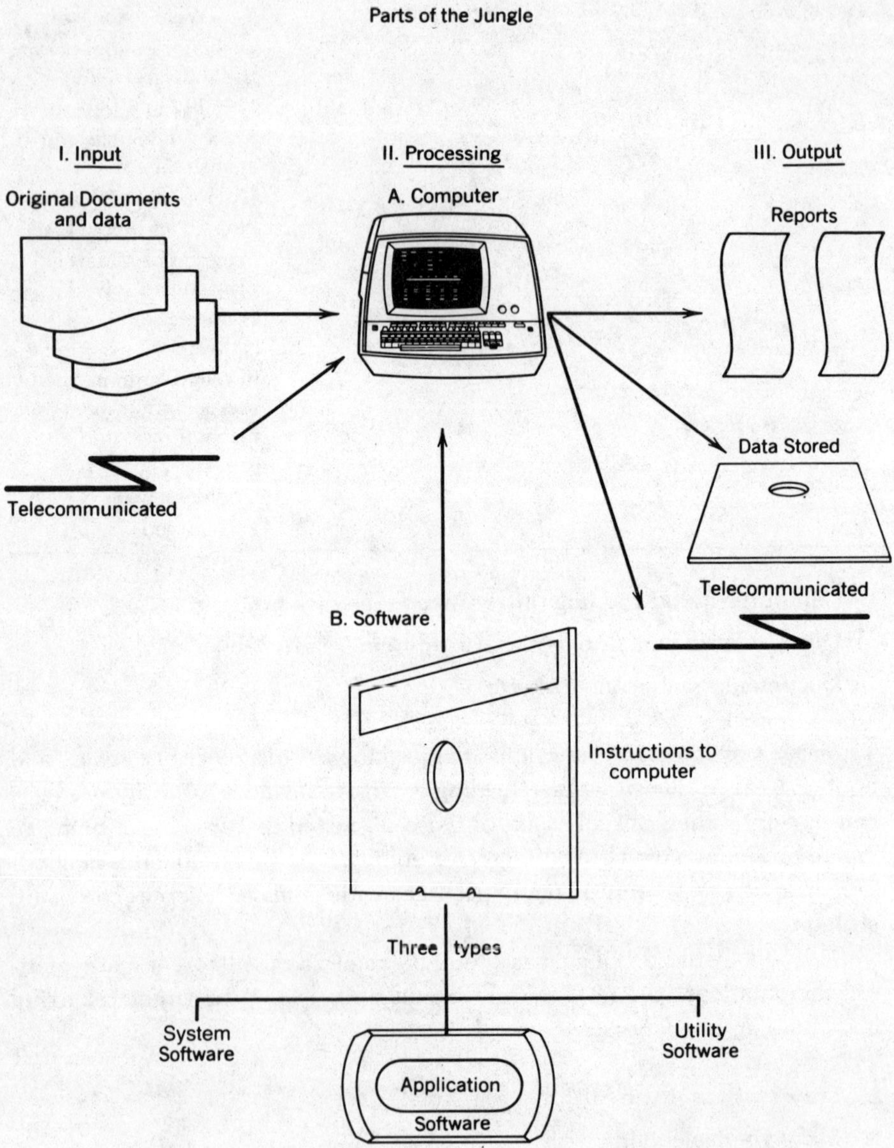

FIGURE 1-1 Microcomputer Overview: Where Application Software Fits

Buy a microcomputer.

Get trained on it.

Be prepared to use it.

Don't apply it in a pressure situation (the software becomes the problem instead of the solution).

A MAP THROUGH THE MICROCOMPUTER MAZE

This book encompasses the software (application programs) that you normally work with. The following displays where this type of software fits in relation with the total computer system.

YOU ARE THE DRIVER

THE COMPUTER IS THE CAR

THE SOFTWARE IS THE FUEL

Software will drive the machine at your direction within certain package limitations.

Hardware	("Iron")
+Software	("Logic")
+Information	("Data")
=System	("Data Processing")

FIGURE 1–2 The Components of a Computer System

The following expands on Figure 1–2 of what is hardware and what is software. Figure 1–3 expands on the connection between hardware and the main types of software.

I. Hardware
  A. Processing units by size (CPU–Central Processing Units)
    1. Large (Mainframe)

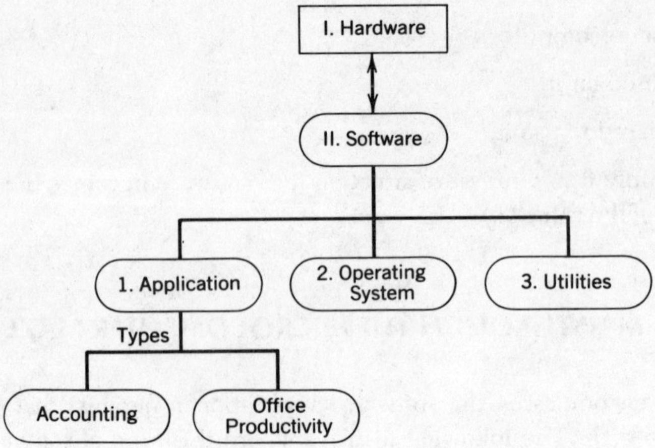

FIGURE 1-3 Microsoftware Programs

(a) Super mainframe
(b) Mainframe
(c) Small mainframe

2. Medium (Minicomputer)
   (a) Super minicomputer
   (b) Mini
   (c) Micro-mini
3. Small (Microcomputer)
   (a) Supermicro (multiuser and 32 bit)
   (b) Micro
   (c) Personal computer
   (d) Home

B. Micro Input Devices
   1. Keyboards and terminals
   2. Mouse
   3. Barcode reader or OCR readers:
      Light pens
      Card readers
      Hand-held laser scanners
   4. Optical word scanners for word input
   5. Writing pads
   6. Modems—remote or online

7. Direct cable
8. Voice

C. Micro Output Devices

1. Printers

   Typewriters
   Dot matrix
   Letter quality
   Laser printers

2. Plotters
3. Tape backup units
4. External floppies or hard disk
5. Terminals
6. Modems—remote or online
7. Direct cable
8. Voice

D. Boards for microcomputer that increase power

1. Additional memory—64K to 256K to 512K to 640K, and so forth.
2. Speed-up boards that increase speed of an IBM PC/XT to 80286 speed from the 8088. The 286 significantly speeds up calculation of spreadsheets, operation of database and wordprocessing packages. Board to increase to 386.
3. Graphics
4. Clocks
5. Encryption
6. Micro-mainframe or Micro-minicomputer links
7. Color
8. Multitasking or Multiuser.

II. Business software

Software is the invisible instructions to the computer (hardware) and is the key to successful computer utilization. Figure 1–3 outlines this microsoftware.

THESE THREE TYPES OF SOFTWARE WORK TOGETHER

1. Application software (see Table 1–2)

   Office productivity

   Accounting

2. Operating system software (CPM™, MS-DOS™, UNIX™, ZENIX™)
Performs essential controlling functions between the application software and the computer. It is similar to a translator so the computer can understand the application software.

Functions:

Controls all system resources

Performs the functions common to all application programs

Provides data management facilities

Performs system checks

3. Utility software
Performs basic housekeeping or general functions for different types of application software
Functions:

Disk format (preparing a diskette to accept information)

Disk copy

File copy

Move file

File reorganization

Erase file

Issues

All three types of software work to allow the user to enter information and perform functions.

Each type may be produced by a different vendor.

Usually one type is not explained in the others' documentation.

Solutions

Reference cards (see Chapter 11) to tie together the various commands that must be used by the same person using the three types of software

Training using a tutorial

User should review the software manuals as well as the hardware manuals.

Application software (see Figure 1–4) is what the user commonly interacts with. It is the workhorse of the computer system. The hardware and the

TABLE 1–2 Major Microcomputer Business Application Software

Office Productivity		Accounting	
Internal Applications	External Communications (General)	Horizontal	Vertical (Industry Specific)
Examples	Examples	Examples	Examples
Electronic spreadsheet	Networking Telecommunications	General Ledger	CPA
			Auditing and EDP audit
	File transfer		CPA:client write-up
Graphics	Terminal Emulation	Accounts receivable	Banking back office
Word handling	Access to external		
Word processing	data bases	Accounts payable	Construction
Thesaurus			
Spell checking			
Report writers		Payroll	Farming
Data base management	External data bases	Inventory	Legal office
List managers	Technical research		
Data base managers	Accounting	Fixed assets	Manufacturing
Sophisticated DBMS	Legal		
	Tax		
Graphics	Informational	Human resource	Medical:Physician office
	News		
Project Management	Stocks	Order entry	Property management
	Public Co. Data	Tax preparation	
Calendar Management			Retail: Point of sale
Scheduling	Specialty	Time and billing	Wholesale distribution
Memory Resident			

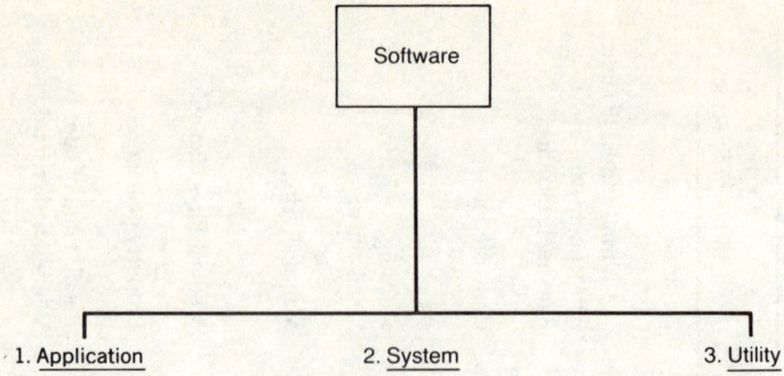

FIGURE 1–4 Major Microcomputer Business Software Applications

other two types of software—system and utilities—provide a foundation for using the micro technology. System software can certainly allow more than one user to have access to the computer. However, it is access to what? The application software provides the instructions to the system to do the specific task of the user whether it is accounting, word processing, or analysis with rows and columns on an electronic spreadsheet. Without this everything else can sit (on the table or in the closet).

Microcomputers can do only so much. Controls have always been the cornerstone of financial information. The underlying theme in producing reliable financial records or analysis is to have internal controls in place. In the rush to revolutionize and use the new microcomputer technology, the basic principle of adequate internal controls is many times ignored. The software or the computer may be powerful; however, outside controls, a methodology for utilization, and planning are musts. There are inherent problems in the use of micros even if edits of the information being entered exist. Some of these problems are:

Input is incorrect and cannot be corrected automatically by computer.

A bad manual system may still exist that significantly affects the microcomputer data.

Bad information can be proliferated faster by the microcomputer.

Information in the computer will be incorrect if original input was/is:

Incorrect

Entered incorrectly

Posted incorrectly

Manipulated improperly later

Output often depends on the degree of individual user training.

Controls may be nonexistent due to former use of data processing department.

Only designated number of transactions can exist.

Only certain dollar values can be entered, stored, and reported.

Speed of micro in larger accounting production mode may be slow.

Diskettes used on most micros are vulnerable to damage.

Incorrect or different data is being used in different departments of the same company. For example, all persons buy their own micro, and enter their own information. As a result, data bases in different departments may not match anymore. Numbers in the marketing department may differ from those in the accounting or the financial analysis departments.

MIS manager or DP manager is not included in buying or utilizing micros. No coordinated effort means different machines are bought; as a result, the software cannot be integrated, causing incompability.

Number of edit features is limited as compared to software packages on much larger computers.

There are size restrictions on storage.

There is less tendency to install controls, because the equipment is relatively inexpensive.

Information can be easily lost, misfiled, or erased.

There is vulnerability to electrical surges and other power problems.

Bugs or problems may exist even in the best software. It has been said if the software is bug-free, it is obsolete.

Rapid changes create quick obsolescence.

The magical box has been opened to the world. This is the real revolution. There is no returning or putting the genie back in the box.

The great advantage to the micro is its ability to put computer power into the hands of the nondata processing people quickly. However, uncontrolled usage can get out of hand. Have we given everyone a live wire or have we grounded it and made it safe? Effective ways to utilize the basics of business software capacity are required. Whether using electronic spreadsheets or an accounts receivable package, controls and planning are essential. These items are not dependent on the next release of software. There is also a credibility gap which claims:

If it is a handwritten financial report, it may not be true.

If it is a typed financial report, it may be true.

If it is a computer-generated report, it must be true!

Actually the reverse may be true!

This compounds the problem and causes real concern in this area.

The so-called microcomputer revolution, which is in fact an evolving technological phenomena, will slow if there exists (1) an inability to properly and productively integrate this technology in a real way to the specific business environment, and (2) an inability for the technology to be utilized and controlled by the only person who can—the individual user.

Those software packages that are very simple, such as stand-alone electronic spreadsheets and word processing, penetrated business quickly, but even they are not used effectively in many cases. For example, one specific task is accomplished while the rest of the package's productivity capabilities are neglected. The integrated office productivity packages and accounting packages, even though not much more expensive, are not the fast sellers. Frequently, people expect the micros to be automatically usable and no training needed to use the software. Great strides are being made in this area and the trend will continue. However, the good and the bad of this technology is that its use rests on the individual user. Normally, an expert or consultant is not involved in the installation or the training. The reason for the micro impact in business is its ease of use. However, realistically there are always certain constraints at any point in time. Each business is different. The micro is incredible technology; however, the boundaries of its abilities must be known and considered.

When the automobile was introduced, people did not expect it to drive itself. Government requires that training take place before a person is licensed to drive. The same emphasis on training has not taken place with the microcomputer. Expectations many times are too high. The problem of integrating software effectively is also compounded by the massive amount of new software and the fast pace of continuing change. One must decide on the software that will do the best job and then concentrate on working with it first—not continually evaluate the next window. The third generation of micro users is here.

1. The first generation users consisted of hobbyists and technical people.
2. The second generation users were daring people of all different backgrounds trying to apply the new technology to their specific needs. Many succeeded and many failed. Many never became friends with their computer. Others started to believe that the computers were unfriendly and many times downright hostile. Frequently, attitude as much as anything else breeded success—a willingness to work it out.
3. The third generation users (a broad base of people) hear the good and the bad connected with the computer. This also includes corporate users of all types. Many of these people were first and second generation users.

Suggestions for the third generation user's enlightenment:

1. Realize that there are pitfalls as well as benefits.
2. Recognize the need for controls outside the computer, training, and utilization of consultants.
3. Establish realistic expectations to determine what technology is really available and what technology is still on the fringes of experimentation.
4. Apply the specific software to your situation productively so that your expectations are met and a satisfactory return on your investment is obtained.
5. Recongnize that in many organizations the MIS (management information systems) director will and should be assisted by a facility microcoordinator or the information may be MIA (missing in action).
6. Create freedom in guidelines for the individual; so new advances are not lost.
7. Use consultants and knowledgeable computer people to help.
8. Create an attitude that the computer has to be used and used successfully.
9. Be patient and reasonable in your expectations.

There are always trade-offs in using microsoftware. Many users do not want controls imposed on them because of its individualistic approach. They want to continue doing business as usual.

TABLE 1–3 Examples of Trade-offs in Microsoftware

Feature	Advantages	Disadvantages
Menu driven Structure	Never gets lost Knows where to go in the system	May have to go through several screens to get to the one you need, such as a report screen
Interactive	Checks and edits for each entry	May be slower in large transactions May work better in batch.
Passwords	Limits access to information	May be a hindrance in a very small organization if diskettes are physically controlled. May be difficult to get around if forgotten.
Compiled program Code	Protects code from unauthorized changes and is faster	If programming problems exist; user does not have access to the code, to correct it.
Stop user to get into file maintenance part of program	Protects from changes in permanent file records	Operators may object to it, can create less flexible systems.
Double entry	Creates a standard in accounting debits and credits	May want to enter all debits, then add result to post the credit.
Ease of use	Helps new people use the system	Can slow down an experienced user considerably. Not being able to move around on the screen or get to the right menu immediately slows the process

Actually ease of use or user friendly takes on a different meaning for each user.

PART TWO

SOFTWARE THAT COUNTS

2

ELECTRONIC SPREADSHEET AGE

ELECTRONIC SPREADSHEET

English Instructions to Computer

Electronic spreadsheet software was and still is one of the main catalysts of the microcomputer age. It has the ability to electronically manipulate numbers, letters, and formulas in a columnar and row (matrix) format. It represents the personal freedom the microcomputer has provided. Its uses in financial decision-making are limited only by the imagination. It is as if there were a paper and column worksheet built into a typewriter with calculating and storage ability. Whatever can be done using a columnar pad can be done using an electronic spreadsheet. The preestablished mathematical, computational ability combined with the printing, formatting, and other abilities literally puts an unending power at the fingertips. Its utilizations run from functioning as a simple memo writer to producing a complex financial model for a five-year business plan.

The functions are almost self-evident. Imagine entering numbers and words on a 10-column piece of paper and then seeing them dance around at your desire to different positions for different assumptions. Just like programming, it becomes a logical approach in instructing the computer to perform functions you want, the way you want, with the data you want. It is real programming and data entry at the same time. Think about it. The mathematical formulas look like BASIC programming commands. The block reference ablility to draw from another block is like a GOTO statement in programming with the ability to tell the computer what to do. It really is a simplified language for the nonprogrammer. That is why it is so powerful. It makes available to laypeople the power of the computer that was once the holy ground only for programmers. It takes the mystery out of instructing computers using a free-flowing worksheet format. By using English with a few understandable commands, program-like instructions are made.

Electronic spreadsheets perform:

Basic math functions

Word storing functions

Input and output with ease

You can enter numbers in almost all the blocks, then use formulas that can compute various financial functions.

Budgeting

Return on investments

Income tax computations

Sales projections

Then based on one number in a block changing, the spreadsheet can automatically recalculate an answer. An example is a sales forecast created from assumptions of:

1. Units to be sold
2. Average price per unit
3. Assumed margin on each unit

What if:

1. Average price of product went down by 10 percent
2. Sales region two is closed
3. Margin increases by 50 percent

What Is a Spreadsheet?

An electronic spreadsheet is software that allows information to be entered into a block that is part of a row-or column-formatted display. It is just as in a 10-column spreadsheet where numbers and words can be entered into a grid format. Columns and rows create the structure of the screen for inputting and for report generation. What you enter is what you get plus much more. Figure 2–1 shows a screen for a typical spreadsheet. Besides numbers and words, other data such as formulas and signs can be entered into blocks. These blocks (also called cells) are designated by the horizontal and vertical axes, such as A2 or B10, just as on a map with longitude and latitude. The flexibility and movability of the electronic spreadsheet make these locations important. You can easily move around in the spreadsheet or jump to a specific block.

Although on the surface it looks like a columnar paper pad, its built-in powers provide a vast range of possibilities. Before and after using these powers, it still retains its rows and columns look. Even within this context, a world of possible uses exists. The columns and rows create a structure for

Block Number
Flashing Light
A B C D E F G H
1
2
3
4
5
6
7
8
9
10
11
12
13
14
15
16
17
18
19
20

FIGURE 2–1 Typical Spreadsheet Screen

entry, edits, and utilization. It is not like a menu-driven general ledger where there is a maintenance file, an entry routine for daily transactions, and a period ending routine.

How commands and information are entered:

"Information entered" or commands available on top line on certain software and others on bottom.

Lotus: Blinking light at top of column numbers with current colum shown

Supercalc: Current column width, memory left, last column/row shown. Then on the next line is the place for entry or entering slash (command menu screen).

For both Lotus and Supercalc, a "/" is entered on entry lines to bring up preestablished commands. Without a "/" numbers, words, or formulas are typed and then entered into an appropriate referenced block.

These spreadsheets certainly are not limited to one set of 10 columns by 40 rows. Based on the storage of the machine (memory) the number of rows and columns can be huge and not unwieldy as it would be on paper or on a number of papers. They can still be viewed on a screen by moving to a specific part of the spreadsheet column. Column P instead of A can be on the left side, or row 200 instead of 0 can be the first row at the top of the screen.

On the command or entry line may be the following:

1. Current block reference—the letter and number that you are on (cell part of worksheet)
2. Information being entered
3. Commands and subcommands available (working similar to menu and submenu routines)
4. Width of column
5. Memory remaining in computer for additional information

Electronic spreadsheet software is in a group of software packages by which the user can instruct the computer by commands. Figure 2–2 indicates a pyramid concept of user-defined software flexibility.

Programming languages are used to instruct the computer. They tell the computer how to operate. The microworld needed tools that allowed some of this instructional ability without the long training time. Hence, software like microcomputer spreadsheets, databases, list managers, and others were developed.

The nonprogrammer now can obtain some of the same programmming

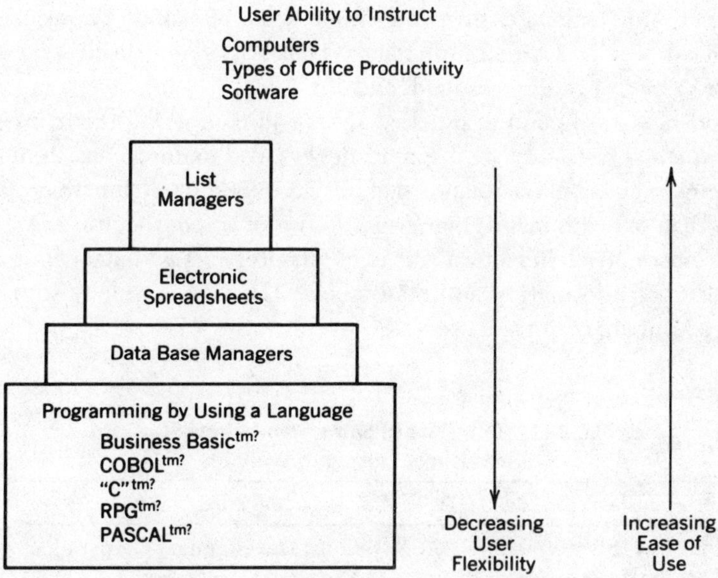

Pyramid of shrinking flexibility of specific types of software packages.

FIGURE 2-2 User Ability To Instruct: Computers/ Types of Office Productivity Software

power. The pyramid in Figure 2–2 is a simplistic view of the learning time weighed against the flexibility of the instructions. The popularity of the spreadsheet is due to its instructional flexibility and short training time as compared to learning a programming language or a data base system.

Spreadsheets are in a group of software called memory resident. Compared to accounting software, all of its data must be stored in the memory of the computer available when it is on. This is the reason why so many users increase their microcomputer memory from 64K to 256K to 512K to 640K to 1.2 meg and so on. Those who are heavy users often upgrade their machines to 640K.

Other memory resident software is available that also requires part of this memory while the computer is on. This increases the need for this type of memory. Previously, you could find minicomputers that had only 32K of memory.

Electronic spreadsheets are not the answer to everything. There are areas where spreadsheets should be used and others where databases should be used, each in its own place.

Programming languages give you a great deal of flexibility; however, they can be used only by trained individuals. Data bases require structured files and time to master their commands and structure.

Spreadsheets are good at quick analysis and computing recurring analyses. Templates, preestablished spreadsheets saved under a consistent name, and macros, a string of commands that provides for a single function made up of more than one command, increase the ease of spreadsheet use. An example of a macro and where to use it is in Chapter 6. List managers assist in storing lists of information and mail labels. They are normally simple and structured but are of limited use.

TABLE 2–1 Examples of Some Stand-alone Standard Spreadsheet Packages Available

Spreadsheet Package	Software Company
Lotus 1-2-3 tm	Lotus Development Corporation
Multiplan tm	Microsoft Corporation
Supercalc tm	Computer Associates

Power of the Electronic Spreadsheet

Electronic spreadsheets are a flexible, creative tool for the user. With little knowledge of computers, a person can utilize the spreadsheet effectively and productively. This software is not based on long charts of accounts, customer files, or some other set-up of master files. It is not as structured as accounting software. By entering numbers, you can use them mathematically in practically any way you want. More powerful than 20 calculators, faster than a speeding slide rule, these spreadsheets can make us all financial analysis superbeings in minutes.

The important concept of the electronic spreadsheet is its ease of use for creating great productivity quickly. The "What If" analysis has catapulted electronic spreadsheet software above practically all others in its financial analysis productivity. The concept is to set up a spreadsheet for a particular situation, like a budget, then to change it based on different assumptions. "What if" sales increased 20%. "What if" cost of goods sold increased by 16%.

The electronic spreadsheet allows one key assumption in a detailed, five-year profit and loss forecast for five subsidiaries to be changed and the recalculated net income to appear immediately. Financial projections based on many different factors are very time-consuming. For example, these are factors that should be considered in each spreadsheet.

1. Assumptions
2. Formulas for spreadsheets
3. Relationships of one item (e.g., expense or revenue) to another

Each spreadsheet software commonly has four main characteristics.

MAIN AREAS CHARACTERISTIC OF A SPREADSHEET

I. *Entry*
 Enter by block—column and row
 Two types of entry possibilities:
 A. Data:
  Letters for words or numbers for numerical data
 B. Functions:
  Symbols for mathematical formulas, commands relating to spreadsheets, and other built-in functions.

II. *Functional Commands*
 Functional instructions, commands, or formatting procedures. These include printing, displaying, and formatting worksheet.
 Spreadsheets provide for a list of functions to be displayed just as in a menu program. It lists the main function first and then the subfunctions (menus and submenus). The main function could be to format the spreadsheet and the subfunction could be to display all numbers in two digits.

III. *Operational Commands*
 A. Basic Mathematics
 B. Logic
  More than
  If—then
 C. Trigonometric
  Square root
  Tangent
 D. Financial
  Rate of return
  Present value

E. Operators
Count
Sum of values
Averaging

IV. *Facilities*

Besides entry of data and built-in commands already listed, different facilities exist. It is the use of specific predesignated function keys that allow:

On-line editing (in Lotus the F2 key is used to edit a block)
Moving the cursor
Setting up commands or formulas
Help facility—provides on-line information concerning a specific built-in command or function condensed from the documentation
Go-to a specified block
Keyboard macros (user-defined series of functions)

The power of the spreadsheet is that it allows for preparing simple to complex applications. Examples are shown in Table 2–2.

Spreadsheet software has certain characteristics that create greater productive power than more structured accounting software. Some of these are listed in Table 2–3. However, accounting software normally provides for greater controls than are found within spreadsheet software. Otherwise they may not be able to be compared in many ways.

TABLE 2–2 Simple to Complex Applications

Simple	Complex
Adding sales numbers and storing them	Internal rate of return of a plant
Basic use of arithmetic functions and word processing abilities	Complex mathematical relational formulas, block formations, and conditional statements.
Suggesting quick application of basic features and commands quickly learned	Continued learning of different functions to facilitate their more sophisticated use and greater use for modeling and reporting from newer applications

TABLE 2–3 User Freedom in Different Types of Software

Freedom of Electronic Spreadsheets	Structure of Accounting and Other Types of Structured Software
1. Setup and productive use	1. Setup and productive use
a. Learning curve for use is hours	a. Training may take days
b. Setup is simple and straightforward	b. Setup may require first establishing parameters, master files, and then account files
c. Calculations and information setup as if you were doing it on a piece of paper	c. Required formats and procedures to set up information and data.
2. Input simple	2. Input
a. Input numbers such as writing on a piece of paper	a. Input allowed through certain required formats. More control.
b. Freedom to format numbers and letters as you desire	b. Fixed or limited formats; many fields may not allow alphanumeric characters.
c. Input quickly	c. Input by going through a menu to get to the proper input screen
3. Output flexible	3. Output
a. Ability to print reports many different ways, including showing formats or only answers	a. Reports normally printed as previously set up unless using an office productivity package, or the accounting package has report writer capabilities
b. Ability to print reports based on information stored in spreadsheet plus temporary addition of notes or numbers one time	b. Reports printed based on data in files

Increasing the Power of Electronic Spreadsheets

The initial uses of the electronic spreadsheet were for stand-alone analysis such as in forecasting and budgeting—especially as it related to "What If" analyses. Once a spreadsheet was set up, making a change in one number or an assumption, such as the percentage of cost of goods sold, could cause a whole new forecast to be created. This was very time-consuming before the advent of the electronic spreadsheet, especially if there were:

Many assumptions
Many ratio relationships

TABLE 2–4 Example of the Simple Power of Spreadsheets—What If

Facts	Electronic Spreadsheet	Manually
1. Corporation with five subsidiaries		
2. Five-year forecast for each subsidiary and consolidated for total corporation		
3. Complete set of assumptions based on inter-relationships of one financial factor to another	Create one spreadsheet with formulas	Create many spreadsheets
	Copy five times in additional columns	Multiply appropriate amounts by another and enter manually.
	Create column for consolidating entries	Keep on writing and keep on multiplying and crossfooting
	Create column to total results for whole corporation	Days in the typing pool
4. Produce reports	Minutes	Again, a day of recomputing

Many departments

Many different periods

The spreadsheet provided an essential, efficient tool for this. However, integrating this tool to other types of software increases its power, significantly.

Integrated applications are created through the use of spreadsheets with other office productivity packages and accounting software. An integrated application could include coordinating number calculations with an extensive report that is edited in the word processor. Another example is where general ledger balances could be transferred to a spreadsheet model to be reanalyzed based on more current financial data. Integration offers a whole new set of possibilities and complexities.

Whether stand-alone or integrated, this tool has opened up the computer to more creative usage by the nondata-processing person. Without knowing how to program, anyone with a few simple instructions can build applications suited to a specific analysis or informational need. The usability of electronic spreadsheets comes from their flexibility, features, and functions such as

Preestablished mathematical formulas
Data manipulation for words and numbers
Formatting procedures
Editing options
User-defined printing options
Flexible data storage
Statistical and logical function abilities

The What If analysis is a new buzz word created by the electronic spreadsheet. An example of this is shown in Table 2–4.

As flexible and useful as electronic spreadsheets are, there are limitations to be considered.

1. *Size of spreadsheet*. Limitations of size of many spreadsheets depends on the computer memory. The software program and all the data need to be in the internal memory (memory while the computer is on). Memories in the 64K and 128K size range do not allow many sophisticated spreadsheets to be built. Many accountants have found 256K, 512K, and 640K of memory much more suitable for larger spreadsheets, and some programs require even more.
2. *Errors caused by flexibility*. Entry is totally dependent upon the user. Some software knows what is to be entered into a specific field, such as only numbers, letters, or only fivc digits. Little if any editing is performed automatically

	by the spreadsheet software. It has no idea what it is you want to do; therefore, it is truly dependent on you for control. Accounting software normally has automatic, built-in controls and edits of input.
3. *Additional work caused by flexibility.*	Electronic spreadsheet can act as different types of tools. Other software may be set up and have features for a specific usage such as: Real estate analysis software Tax preparation Audit tools List manager Project manager These features normally make these specific software programs better and faster tools for a specific usage.
4. *Still a microcomputer package.*	Calculators, manual entry into columnar paper spreadsheets, and programmable calculators can be cheaper, more cost effective, and faster approaches for certain situations.
5. *Little security.*	Access to the spreadsheet can be very easy because of few controls. Errors can be made or spreadsheets changed without audit or transaction trails. Previously used spreadsheets need to be used carefully.
6. *Programming limitations despite flexibility*	Spreadsheets can only do so much. They do not allow global changes as in word processors. Sorting is limited (many do not sort by key letters), usually to rows and columns; file structures are not as useful as in

data base managers. Complex statements and functions may be misused or misunderstood. Of course, there are ways to limit these risks and create your own controls.

Ten Most Used Commands in Spreadsheets

1. Retrieve or save a file
2. Recalculate
3. Repeat
4. Copy/Move
5. Global display and recalculation
6. Editing
    - Insert
    - Delete
    - Erase
7. Format
    - Column width
    - Two decimal places for dollars
    - Whole dollars
8. Protect/Unprotect
    - Blocks
    - Columns
    - Rows
9. Printing
    - Sections of spreadsheets
    - Results of formulas
    - Formulas
10. Creating string of commands (MACROS)
    - Through allowable procedures
    - Some called execute commands or keyboard macros

Six-Step Process to Improving Spreadsheets

Step 1. *Plan*. Define the result. Know what you want the spreadsheet to do.

Step 2. *Start Simple*. Prepare simple worksheets first.

Step 3. Build on simple spreadsheets.

Step 4. Create structure for each spreadsheet so it is easier to use, change, and correct

Step 5. Create and define relationships that aid analysis. When applicable, have one number effected by another, instead of entering one each time. The more relationships, the faster data can be entered and the more powerful What If usage can be.

Step 6. Practice and use the spreadsheet. Exercise the various commands and functions. The more it is used the more you understand its functions. Until then, you never really know how many ways you can use the spreadsheet in your work. It is not as in other packages; the information entered does not have to be saved. The integrity of the original analysis is not destroyed. By not saving the exercise spreadsheet or by saving it under a different name, the master spreadsheet is kept intact.

Examples of Time-Saving Tips

1. Partition spreadsheets
   Break up large spreadsheets into smaller functional parts
   Save each part separately as well as in total
   Allow for:
      Building partitions
      Protecting each partition
      Finding errors more easily
      Making changes to spreadsheets faster
2. Place numbers that will change in one section labeled Input, and reference them to the proper cells in the Calculation section and setup separate report (Output) sections:

   a. Input

   b. Calculation

   c. Output

3. Create templates

   a. Create recurring reports such as monthly financial statement analysis. Save the title, column headings, and line description of the analysis (the skeleton) before transferring or entering specific amounts. After the spreadsheet is saved, then enter amounts. Reload the skeleton for the next new financial spreadsheet.

   b. Create recurring analysis such as reconciliation of federal tax expenses to book expenses.

4. Build Template Library

   a. Set of worksheets for tax preparation

   b. Separation of templates by type of spreadsheet:
      Financial analysis
      Tax preparation
      Auditing
      Management reports
      Budgeting and forecasting
      Other spreadsheets

5. Build on other spreadsheets
   Combine similar worksheets
   In analysis for total sales, combine spreadsheet analysis of Product A sales with Product B and Product C. For analysis, use parts of quarterly analysis of annual sales.

6. Buy templates available on the market
      Real estate analysis
      Return on investment
      Tax preparation
      Auditing

7. Pre-established common commands

   a. One formula made up of a string of other single formulas

   b. One command that performs a string of commands

   c. One key that is established to allow certain more specific and powerful functions to take place. (This feature is in many of the spreadsheets.)

8. Plan the structure of a worksheet first. Know what it should look like and review functions of the spreadsheet to take advantage of using it in as many ways as possible.

RECOMMENDATIONS TO AVOID OBVIOUS PROBLEMS

1. Save, save, save. Keep on saving your spreadsheet work; what is not saved is lost.
2. Do not write over a good worksheet.
3. Protect your work from others. Each person using spreadsheets on a computer could use his or her own diskette instead of storing them on a hard disk.
4. Review your work for reasonableness.
5. Always print reports.
   a. Without headings for final management report to be reviewed
   b. With headings, row and column references, and formulas. This way you can quickly find assumptions and change spreadsheets.
6. Share data in spreadsheets and make it part of the common company information. Data for 50 employees pulling information from 50 different sources creates disaster. No one knows what number is correct. Personal freedom for analysis must be controlled at least through utilization of common, correct company data. This is one of the concerns of the personal computer revolution. Basic business decisions should be based on the same available facts. It is easy enough to manipulate facts without starting with different ones.
7. Keep it as simple as possible. If the analysis still belongs on a three-column pad, keep it there, don't get fancy. If a simple spreadsheet will do, then stay away from complex integrated applications. If taking a diskette by hand to another user in another office is easier, then don't transfer by network. If reentering the data to a spreadsheet is easier, then don't use file or spreadsheet combine commands or a sophisticated general ledger—spreadsheet transfer. Use what works best for your business.
8. Use special, separate function packages to audit flow of formulas and to document total formula no matter what block they may be in.

9. Use protect command, hidden cell features (in Lotus), or compile (compilation is done by a compiler program performed by a qualified person) standard templates to be used again by yourself or others.
10. Use same spreadsheet throughout organization. This spreadsheet should be reviewed by a central department or person before distribution.

CONTROLS

In using an electronic spreadsheet for financial work, controls become very important. These include controls over input, edit checking, output, and storage. These same controls are considered when accounting software is developed. Therefore they should also be considered when developing spreadsheets.

Examples of these are:

A. Input

1. Provide for one section of the worksheet for input of all data.
2. Show all assumptions that are being used and other pertinent facts in one area.
3. Make sure macros and required formulas are protected in some way so they cannot be deleted by mistake by deleting a whole row or column or some other simple function.

B. Edit checking

1. Use formulas that both perform the mathematical function and can edit them. An example of this is footing a column and a row that has the same answer residing in the same block. This is done manually by crossfooting the column and row on a workpaper. Many of us have done this to check our addition to make sure we get the same answer in both directions. However, in electronic spreadsheets, normally the row or column is summed by adding the row of numbers or the column. Even electronically, summing in one direction could produce the wrong result.

As a specific example, say we are using Lotus and the total for the spreadsheet is in block D11.

• Many users would create this by summing only the numbers in the column or the numbers in the rows.
"@ SUM (D1.D10)" or
"@ SUM (A11.C11)."

• Instead of summing one way use a crossfact formula.

• This formula could be—
"If (@ SUM (D1.D10) = @ SUM (A11.C11), @ SUM (D1.D10), @ ERR)"

This if statement says—
• Look at Row total = column total
• If equal print total
• If not "ERR".

Another editing approach would be to put the total of D1 to D10 in block D11. Then put the total of A11 to C11 in block E11. Finally, put the difference between block D11 (total of columns) and block E11 (total of rows) in block G11 and put in block F11 the word Difference. In this way you see the total of both directions.

2. Put a formula in the spreadsheet that reviews the totals or each number in the spreadsheet and compare it to another edit amount. Basically this can be a check to determine that amounts in the worksheet are reasonable.

   An example of this is a company having annual sales of $2 million and preparing a sales analysis by product. A formula (or formulas) could be created to check the blocks and determine none is over $2 million.

C. Output

1. Print both answers and formulas.
2. Use macros that will print the proper blocks of the spreadsheet each time.
3. Print both row and column reference on one of the printouts.
4. Those spreadsheets that are being used for recurring reports or used by many people should be reviewed by a specific person or department before their utilization. In addition, output should be reviewed

by someone other than the user to compare them to the original spreadsheet and make sure no changes were made to the formulas or other key areas.

D. Storage

1. A consistent naming convention for all your spreadsheets should be made up before naming any spreadsheets. Retrieving spreadsheet files after building a number of spreadsheets can become difficult. An example is naming all budget spreadsheets Bud, then the month and year (e.g. BUDJ88—Budget for January 1988).
2. Use different disks for different types of spreadsheets. An example is one disk for budgets and one for actual financial results.
3. Print out a directory of the spreadsheet files on the disks periodically and put it with the disks. In this way you can find the disk you need much faster.
4. Put the purpose of the worksheet in block A1.
5. Each worksheet should be saved under its own name, then under a different name on the same diskette. For example, a spreadsheet named BUDGET should be saved as BUDGETB for Budget Backup file.
6. All spreadsheets should be saved on another diskette periodically.
7. If using a hard disk, spreadsheet files should be saved on disks logically and then erased from the hard disk when no longer needed.

3

INTEGRATING AND USING SPREADSHEET POWER

INCREASING HORIZON OF SPREADSHEET SOFTWARE

Electronic spreadsheet software has captured the enthusiasm of all. The stand-alone electronic spreadsheet has a wide range of potential uses. The range of uses and users expands even more through the tie-in of this tool to other software. The sharing of data makes each tool more powerful than when used alone.

In understanding these tie-ins, the basic structure of the different types of software should be reviewed. One way to structure business software is shown in the following table. Electronic spreadsheets (upper lefthand corner) can be integrated with the software in its own column and in all other columns displayed. It has become a common bond between software. The microcomputer has created this new bond more than any other type of hardware.

In this chapter and others certain new microcomputer buzzwords are used. Chapter 16 provides books that list the most common buzzwords and define them. This book was not intended to do that. However, some of the words used in this chapter are defined below. These are:

Templates
Modeling
Macros
Memory resident software

MAJOR MICROCOMPUTER BUSINESS SOFTWARE APPLICATIONS POWER THROUGH DATA TRANSFER AND SOFTWARE INTEGRATION

Office Productivity		Accounting	
Internal Applications	External Communications	Horizontal (General)	Vertical (Industry Specific)
Examples	Examples	Examples	Examples
Electronic spreadsheet	Networking Telecommunica-	General Ledger	CPA
	tions		Auditing and EDP audit
	File transfer		CPA:client write-up
Graphics	Terminal Emulation	Accounts receivable	Banking back office
Word handling	Access to external		
Word processing	data bases	Accounts payable	Construction
Thesaurus			
Spell checking			
Report writers		Payroll	Farming
Data base management	External data bases	Inventory	Legal office
List managers	Technical research		
Data base managers	Accounting	Fixed assets	Manufacturing
Sophisticated DBMS	Legal		
	Tax		
Graphics	Informational	Human resource	Medical:Physician office
	News		
Project Management	Stocks	Order entry	Property management
	Public CO Data	Tax preparation	
Calendar Management			Retail: Point of sale
Scheduling	Speciality	Time and billing	Wholesale distribution
Memory Resident			

Templates and modeling have become common buzzwords in this area. Templates are previously saved spreadsheets that normally are designed to be used a number of times. Many times they are set up with specific blocks blank or specific blocks that should be changed to derive new variations of the old spreadsheet. We used to think of a template as a tool for drawing flow charts. Now they are predesigned worksheets. Modeling normally revolves around templates; however, these are created to duplicate a specific business situation, even though it is very difficult to do so in numbers alone.

To create templates, models, and more sophisticated spreadsheet usage the macro capability exists in spreadsheets. This is the ability to string commands together. One key can represent a set of commands that leads to an action. Normally the menu and submenu structure of the software is followed to provide all the instructions to the computer. In using macros, you can build this set of instructions so only one key is necessary instead of following the menu structure to accomplish an action. An example of this is the instructions to print part of the worksheet. This command can be built in a macro so it can be used instead of following the menu command structure each time you want to print the same row and column setting. Some examples of macros are in Chapter 6 (The Manager's Search For a Word Processor).

A new type of software being used with spreadsheets are concurrent memory resident software. These are packages, normally shown in part of the screen, that can be used at the same time you are in another software package. The important use is that you can be in the spreadsheet software while able to use the commands and features of a totally different software package. An example is using Lotus while able to bring up a small window on the screen to enter notes or perform DOS commands. All of this can be done without leaving Lotus 1-2-3. Examples of these types of packages are discussed in this chapter as important tools to increasing the power and ease of use of spreadsheet software.

Users can choose from four basic levels of electronic spreadsheet usage and integration.

Tools That Expand Power of Spreadsheet Interfaced Tools—Type 2

Besides the individual spreadsheet software package (Type 1), other packages have been developed around the spreadsheet to offer other important facets of ability to the user. In the case of the popular spreadsheet Lotus 1-2-3,

Type	*Description*	*Product Examples**
1. Stand-alone	Spreadsheets—some with limited capacities	Lotus 1-2-3 Javelin Multiplan Supercalc
2. Interfaced tools	Tools—share data in electronic spreadsheet files	Companion Lotus products: Lotus Hal 1-2-3 Reportwriter Lotus Graphwriter Lotus Freelance Spotlight Add-on Products by other vendors: IQ—Intelligent Query Note-It Sidekick Sideways SQZ! The Spreadsheet Auditor What's Best
3. Total integrated office software tool	Office software packages working with each other as a common menu. Tools normally include: electronic spreadsheet, word processing, data base, graphics, and communications	Decision Maker Framework Symphony PFS: First Choice
4. Office tool to accounting software	Office productivity tools working with accounting packages	Connection of Lotus 1-2-3 to G/L, A/P, A/R, Payroll, and Inventory

*Products Trademarked

specific packages have been developed that can work as an integral part of using Lotus.

Some software packages were developed by Lotus Development Corporation itself, each adding another feature or dimension upon the basic electronic spreadsheet. They can become integral tools in using Lotus 1-2-3. These tools both simplify and expand the use of the spreadsheet. Some are memory resident software, which is explained in Chapter 9.

Examples of these are:

I. Companion Lotus products—By Lotus Development Corporation (not all of their products are listed)
   A. Lotus Hal—Of all the products this is one is the most important and powerful add-on tool.
      1. Uses English phrases to provide for easier and faster use of Lotus 1-2-3 for both the new and experienced user. For example:
         a. Use the name of cells to create totals, instead of using cell references. Command can be "total Jan to Dec."
         b. Graph amounts using simple English commands.
         c. Use English phrases to create Macros.
      2. User can "undo" the previous command. For example:
         a. If previous command was to erase a cell, then you see this was a mistake, you can bring back the erased cell.
         b. If cells are moved to the wrong places, user can go back to the positions that previously existed.
      3. List formula.
      4. List relationships between cells.
      5. User can combine cells easily.
   B. 1-2-3 Report Writer—A report writer for Lotus 1-2-3.
   C. Lotus Graphwriter—Can take data from Lotus 1-2-3 and turn it into a sophisticated chart or graph presentation. Provides presentation capabilities above the graphing of Lotus 1-2-3 itself. Product has specific predesignated charts and graphs.
   D. Lotus Freelance—This is a graphic package that can be used on its own or in conjunction with Graphwriter above. It provides for production of forms, signs, maps, graphs, and many other presentations. It can pull in data from Lotus 1-2-3.
   E. Spotlight—This product can be used while being in Lotus 1-2-3, without the need to get out of Lotus. It can act as a:

1. notepad
2. appointment book
3. calculator
4. index card file

One example of use is putting in cell references and listing assumptions for them without getting out of the spreadsheet.

The above products can of course be used for many purposes other than a tie to the Lotus spreadsheet.

II. Add-on products (see Chapter 9) by other vendors—examples of some of these.

A. IQ-Intelligent Query—By Programmed Intelligence Corporation. This is a reportwriter that will use data from Lotus 1-2-3 spreadsheets and turn them into sophisticated reports. It will also attach to other products, such as data base software.

B. Note-It—By Turner Hall Publishing. This provides for the Lotus 1-2-3 user the ability to attach notes to specific cells. It is another memory resident software that can be used at the same time the user is in the spreadsheet. It is very important to financial personnel, as it enables them to provide specific assumptions and other important references included. Many times spreadsheets are in a budget report, and a separate nonreferenced assumption list is shown. This disjointed approach is much less understandable and much more likely to be misunderstood.

C. Sidekick—By Borland International. This allows you to make notes while using Lotus 1-2-3. It is a memory resident software. It has a calendar, a notepad where cell assumptions can also be listed, and many other easy features. It can appear in a small box in the upper right corner of the screen while the remaining spreadsheet is still displayed.

D. Sideways—By Funk Software. This provides for printing spreadsheets on their sides instead of straight up and down. It allows you to avoid taping wide spreadsheets together. Many spreadsheets can be printed sideways in one piece when they cannot be printed up and down. One example is a budget spreadsheet that has column A for line descriptions, the next 12 columns for the months, and the last column for totals. Many times this can be printed sideways but not the other way. In financial spreadsheets this is very helpful.

E. SQZ! Data Squeezer For Lotus—By Turner Hall Publishing. Data in a Lotus file is squeezed together to provide for more disk storage, and

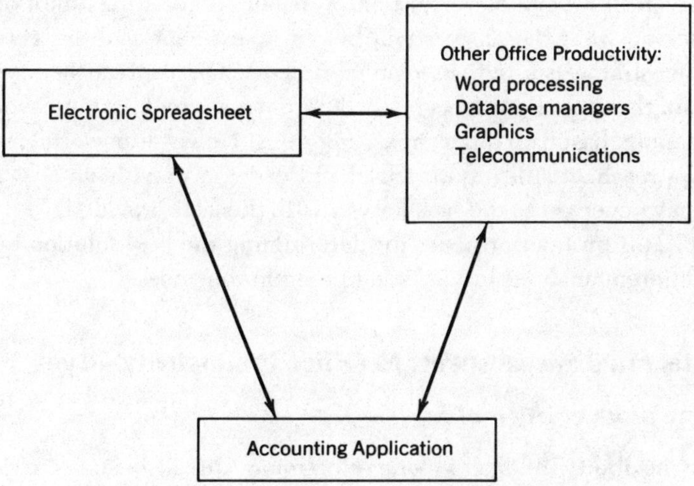

Combining countries to create a world of software.

FIGURE 3–1 Integrated Spreadsheet—Office Productivity Tool

less time retrieving and saving files. It is especially useful when storing large spreadsheets on disks. It also has password protection for Lotus Version 1 and 1A. The password feature is in Lotus Version 2.

F. The Spreadsheet Auditor—By Consumers Software Inc. Many different audit techniques for spreadsheets are available in this software. Too often it is difficult to trace problems in a spreadsheet or audit them. When spreadsheets become the basis of important financial analysis or are used as a recurring worksheet in a CPA firm, this product can be very valuable. Features include:

    Cross-reference by cell, function, or range name
    Cell noter
    Sideways printing
    Worksheet map as an approach to spotting quick problems
    Documentation
    Macro analysis
    Many other debugging reports and features

G. What's Best—By General Optimization, Inc. The best solution to a financial or scheduling worksheet can be determined by this program.

The "What If" analysis that electronic spreadsheets allow has given us a very powerful tool in making different assumptions and seeing what the answer will be. In investment analysis, return on investment is a tedious manual process. On a spreadsheet you can run the same basic facts many different ways to determine what may happen based on different assumptions. However powerful this new approach, it still requires trial and error to provide an answer and may never get to the best answer with the facts provided.

This product provides for determining the best solution in many different analyses just as linear programming does.

Integrated Spreadsheets to Office Productivity—Type 3

Total office productivity tool

The user flexibility of stand-alone electronic spreadsheets is expanded through the interactive integration or sharing with other office productivity software. Because one menu can control all of the office productivity tools, a complete data base of information is created.

As previously stated, spreadsheet programs are like English type programming. With added tools additional program abilities are possible, especially relating to data bases.

Electronic spreadsheets working with word processing, graphics, data bases, and telecommunications obtain combinations of

numbers + words = word processing
pictures = graphics
structured numbers + word files = data base manager
communications = telecommunications

The combinations expand the capabilities of spreadsheets into another world of possibilities—electronic spreadsheets being the focal point of the world. By combining all the spreadsheet commands with the specific word handling and data management capabilities of other software, sophisticated activities and continuing analysis can take place. However, with the expanded capabilities go expanded learning curves and implementation time to your project. Many techniques are being and will be created to reduce the time required for start up and implementation of these expanded tools.

For the sophisticated user, the additional capacities far exceed the relatively small additional costs.

TABLE 3–1 Integration Considerations and Specific Example

Capital Budget Example

Three Considerations	Stand-Alone Spreadsheet	Integrated To Accounting
1. Use of specific powers	1. Capital budgeting with "what if" analysis and return on investment	1. Capital budgeting with automated input; appropriate software such as G/L.
2. Productive characteristics	2. Number handling with mathematical formulas built in.	2. Quick input and faster manipulation to answers.
3. Learning curve	3. Quick to learn	3. More to learn, especially how to transfer historical data.

For the novice who will use one or two features of a spreadsheet, the stand-alone tool is very efficient and time effective.

For the accounting department using accounting software, connecting it to the spreadsheet could significantly improve analysis and reporting.

Tie-in to all of the office productivity tools may not be necessary.

Choose carefully. It's your option!

Some of these tools can be sophisticated. Others, like First Choice by PFS, combine word processing to data base to spreadsheet with one simple menu and are designed directly for the first time computer user.

Integrating with Accounting Software—Type 4

Many accounting software vendors connect their software to another company's spreadsheet software. Other times they create their own office productivity packages or privately label others to offer a complete package.

Many vendors provide for their data or files to be connected to Lotus 1-2-3. Data from a General Ledger or Accounts Receivable can be passed to a spreadsheet so a new report can be issued, additional analysis can be performed on the results, a previous analysis can be updated with actual results, or a budget can be compared to actual data.

In Table 3–1 are examples of the combined power, what it can specifically do, and the learning curve to obtain this power. Table 3–2 provides an

TABLE 3–2 Quarterly Management Report

	Integrated Office Productivity Tool and In-House Accounting Software					
Step Description	Electronic Spread	Word Processing	Graph	Database Telecommunications	General Ledger	Accounts Receivable
1. General ledger close on 5th day					1	
2. Financial statements prepared with special comparative analyses	2				1	
3. Prepare separate report which updates annual budget on statement:	2				1	
a. Add actual results Y-T-D with remaining budget for the year						
b. Enter this amount in budget column and take variances						
c. In the middle of the year a comparative to the established annual budget may be meaningless for management information purposes						
4. Prepare report on largest customers and other key facts	2	3	4		1	

Process						
a. Information from accounting systems financial analyses on spreadsheet						
b. Written report on word processing using certain key parts of financials						
c. Provide graphic presentations on such things as product analysis						
5. Ratios	2		3	4	1	
a. Financial information						
b. Financial ratios						
c. Graph ratios						
d. Obtain information from external database						
e. List competition and industry factors maintained in database manager files						
6. Prepare management report	1	2				
7. Send information to those in a list on 10th of month	3	4	5	6	2	1

Numbers in blocks show software needed for each process and order used in example of how a Quarterly Management Report can be produced effectively by using this integrated power.

Many times managers are more interested in where to apply a tool than specifically how it works. After learning the commands, it still does not give automatic insight into where to apply it. In training classes for managers, they ask as many questions about where as to how.

OVERVIEW USING EXAMPLES OF THE COMBINED POWER

Examples of how this combined power works

1. *Budgeting*. Many companies provide a budget as a set of numbers, then another separate budget in written form—two different processes that should be the same. Both budgets are planning to spend the same dollars. The reasons should be connected to the dollars. Many times budgets require much more than just numbers. A narrative is important for understanding. When a budget is submitted, increases in requests for a line item expense normally need justification. This is best done by tying the individual accounting number request to a specific narrative. The budgeting process is an important and extensive process that can be tied together more easily.

   (a) *Numbers* — Numbers detail line item expenses for departments, subsidiaries, and total company.

   (b) *Words* — Words relate restrictions, goals, limitations, and insights.

   (c) *Pictures* — Graphic presentations provide immediate understanding.

   (d) *Communications* — In situations where there are other subsidiaries or plants spread out, budgeting procedures coupled with telecommunications can significantly increase the speed and quality of the production of the budget.

2. *Forecasting*. Forecasts indicate what the future can hold and are often an integral part of a business plan. An integrated program is very useful for producing forecasts.

(a) *Structure*	A data base can be established for: The financing contacts to be made, whether private placements, banks, venture capital, or tax shelter organizations Person to contact Other vital details maintained Addresses
(b) *Communications*	Telecommunicate key information from an external data base and apply to spreadsheet
(c) *Numbers*	Three year forecast in spreadsheet
(d) *Words*	Report on forecast, including key amounts, assumptions, and discussion of what the forecast is
(e) *Pictures*	Graphic representation of past three year financials and three-year forecast

3. *Analysis of a company*.

(a) *Pictures*	Showing graphic presentations
(b) *Structure*	Continuing access to external data bases for industry standard comparisons and public reports of target companies to be compared. Data base recording of these analyses on a continuing basis
(c) *Numbers*	Continually analyzing through different reports and comparisons on electronic spreadsheets

4. *Audit procedure*. Many audit procedures are aided significantly by the combinations of the electronic spreadsheet, graphics, and word processing.

(a) *Audit report*.

Perfect for the integrated tool

Required	*Output*	*Package*
Numbers	Financial statements	Electronic spreadsheet

Numbers and words	Financial statements, ratios, and appropriate management report comments	Spreadsheet calculation and word processing
Words and numbers	Footnotes	Combination of spreadsheets and word processing
Numbers and pictures	Graphic presentations of financial statement ratios	Graphics packages
Words	CPA's Opinion	Word processing with use of blanket reports

(b) All benefited by and needing the power of the integration of the various tools. The items below can be tied to other software.

Lead sheets

Inventory analyses

Accounts receivable confirmations

A/R statistics

(c) Review of financial statements

Numbers	Comparative analysis	Spreadsheet
Structure	Historical data and details	Recorded in data base
Words	Report	Word processing including certain amounts in financial

(d) SEC Statements. This whole process frequently revolves around last minute, late night changes in numbers, words, and graphs. Require double checking of numbers cross-referenced and matched in narrative as well as financial statements, footnotes, and SEC schedules.

Desktop publishing software can also play a role in reducing costs and turnaround time.

5. Record-keeping

   (a) Structure: The existence of a data base significantly improves the ability of office productivity software to act as a simple record-keeping tool. Sophisticated data bases allow these to be written almost as in a programming language. Inventories can be organized, general ledger charts of accounts established, accounts receivable, and accounts payable all simply done.

   (b) Numbers. The reporting by electronic spreadsheet from data base managers.

   (c) Words. Tie-in to dunning letters and reports. Pre-established programs certainly aid when there is a large volume.

6. Pricing model

Structure	Maintain data base of different products and different pricing levels.
Numbers	Spreadsheet of volume/price model possibilities

7. Tax preparation and calculation

Words	Letters on tax returns
Communications	Telecommunications for subsidiary tax return information
Structure	Data base management capabilities for structure of return and analysis of prior returns by line

8. Acquisitions

   Acquisitions analysis improved by graphic presentation and interrelated explanation of numerical analysis, written analysis, and recommendations. The "What If" analysis is important here.

9. Calendar Management and Due Dates Use Data Base Feature in Spreadsheet to:

   (a) Project management

   (b) Telecommunicate calendars to others—organize

   Travel

Meetings

Audits

Shows

10. Cash Flow and Funds Statement

(a) Financial analysis

(b) Variance analysis

(c) Communications back and forth to subsidiaries

(d) Graphic presentations of major sources percentages and uses

Millions More Ideas

The integrated office productivity tool can present an immense capacity from one screen. In the future, it is logical that other major tools will be connected to maintain its total office productivity concept. The examples given indicate just some of the uses for the totally integrated tools over the stand-alone electronic spreadsheet.

Of course, the greater the power for good, the greater the potential for destruction. The more complicated your specific usages, the more careful you should be in maintaining your work and outputting the results. Obviously, the interaction of various tasks requires coordination and control. This becomes very important. Controls outside the computer as well as in the software should be implemented.

TEN IDEAS USING ELECTRIC SPREADSHEETS AND ALL INTEGRATED OFFICE TOOLS

1. Budgeting
2. Forecasting
3. Modeling
4. Acquisition analysis
5. Audit procedures and workpapers
6. Calendar, due dates, and time sheets
7. Cash flow and funds statement analysis
8. Record-keeping simply performed

9. Tax preparation and calculation
10. Word processing, list managers, and other straightforward applications

The items listed above are explained as follows:

1. Budgeting
   a. Capital budgets.
   b. Operating budgets—monthly, quarterly, annually.
   c. Comparison of actual to budgeted with variances displayed.
   d. Comparison of actual to budgeted showing only variances over a certain dollar level. This can be done by using If and Greater—Than statements.
   e. Budgets using interrelationships. Instead of budgeting a specific amount for a specific item, create budgets with one revenue or expense line item based on another.

   Use interrelationships between one line item and another. Of course, simple relationships do not normally exist; however, they can be used to create useful models.

Examples: Budget for a Company

Line Item	*Based on*
Sales	Percent increase over previous year
Sales returns	Percent × Sales
Cost of goods sold	Percent to Sales
Advertising	Percent to Sales
Sales commission	Percent to Sales
Employee fringe benefit	Benefits Percent × Employee salaries
Bad debt expense	Percent to Sales
Income taxes	Percent of pretax income
Interest expense	Percent × Average debt on balance sheet

f. Budgets created by analyzing the line item and relationship to general key factors instead of entering specific amount.

Line Item	*Based On*
Sales	Units × average unit price
Rent	Rental rate × average square footage
Telephone expense	Number of lines × average cost per line and fixed cost
Trade show expense	Per show cost × number of shows
Travel—Sales personnel	Average cost per trip × number of trips (per employee) × Number of sales personnel

2. Forecasting
   a. Sales forecasts.

      Detailed product lines.

      Geographical territories.

      Types of sale—units and pricing information.

      Trend analysis using past history.

      By salesperson.
   b. Order level.
   c. Individual expense items on three–five year forecasts.
   d. People forecasts by skills requirements and projection of the average salary level for that skill to obtain total salaries.
   e. Cash needs requirements.
   f. Inventory levels by type of category or by specific unit, then total.
   g. Analysis beyond simple trends—if seasonal or cyclical, use seasonal statistical variation formula.
   h. Individual expenses.
   i. Forecasting business activity through many different techniques and marketing services.
   j. Forecast can be aided by extrapolating historical trends. However, many items may not follow any trend. Trend analysis can be aided by the least squares method (a statistical method of trend analysis).

Formulas such as these are easy to handle on an electronic spreadsheet. Certain trends could be determined and be very helpful in forecasting. Examples are:

Percentage relationships of one expense to another or to sales could be detected.

Trends in specific product sales and their point in the life cycle of similar products. Trends in bad debt percentage.

Trends in cash collections of a specific account or a group of accounts.

3. Modeling

a. Modeling in general recreates or mathematically analyzes a business situation. It suggests What If? through using a fixed number or a variable. What If? is a situation in which one number in a block is changed, thus altering the total spreadsheet. Modeling can include forecasts and budgets. However, it is normally much more. It has the ability to allow the analysis of many different scenarios in the same business. Before electronic spreadsheets, discussions on modeling were reserved for graduate schools, consultants, and top executives. Now, spreadsheets make modeling real. By using spreadsheets, modeling can be very straightforward, although it still can be a lengthy process. Business numbers that are the input to spreadsheets do not fall into nice little blocks, nor do they fall into nice little formulas. However, the use and reuse of a spreadsheet model can aid in understanding and problem solving if it is used continuously. The final results should be compared to original models to determine what went wrong and thus create better models in the future.

b. The model is a significant catalyst in the analysis of a business situation. Models can take many shapes and forms, from very simplistic to a representation of the whole business structure.

c. In modeling, the What If? can produce financial analyses within three expectations:

Optimistic.

Probable.

Pessimistic.

The expectations provide a range for decision making. Modeling is aided significantly by the integration of the electronic spreadsheets to other tools such as graphics, data bases, and word processing. Modeling is aided by:

Graphics comparing different assumptions.

Data bases storing various information that could be the basis of input to the model.

Words describing assumptions, what is needed, and end results.

d. The use of the pessimistic model might protect the company against unforseen cash flow problems. Examples of such analysis may be

Projecting the costs of a new plant and its expected production date.

Acquiring a new product.

Redeveloping a product.

Selling a product.

Establishing the cost of a fixed bid for a job.

Also, since changing numbers on an electronic spreadsheet is so easy, using the theory of probabilities as an aspect of model becomes realistic. The probabilities in turn give more insight into tracking and gauging results. In addition, graphics add another spectrum of communication and analysis: one picture is worth a thousand words. An example is a graph of expected results in a bar chart with columns headed optimistic, probable, pessimistic.

Probability theory, graphics, and modeling itself provide the increased ability to:

Analyze alternative courses of action.

Communicate recommended course.

Decide on a course.

Track results and compare to expectations.

e. Models can be sophisticated. They can be created from the bottom up or as offshoot to a budget, a forecast, or other spreadsheets. They should be created to be reused. The detailed example in Chapter 5 describes the model building process.

4. Acquisition analysis

a. Capital acquisitions.

Internal rate of return.

Payback.

Net present value.

b. Company acquisition.

Purchase versus pooling of interest.

Allocation of goodwill to specific assets.

Goodwill factors.

Purchasing assets versus purchasing company.

c. Leveraged buyouts.

d. Syndications.

e. Joint research and development projects.

f. Tax shelters.

5. Audit procedures and workpapers

a. Client can build worksheets for auditor if client is using a computer. In this instance, integration of accounting packages and an electronic spreadsheet is very useful (see Chapter 6).

b. Ideas for specific programs.

Listing of audit program.

Alternative procedures.

Due dates.

Personnel resource commitments.

Personnel resources by category.

Lead sheet preparation summarizing chart of accounts classifications.

Bank reconciliation in spreadsheet.

Accounts receivable confirmation listing and resultant statistical analysis of results.

Inventory reconciliations.

Physical to perpetual comparison.

Statistical analysis.

Pricing tests using formulas and templates.

LIFO–FIFO pricing.

Percentage of completion analysis and testing.

Property, plant, and equipment summary:

Detail and testing calculations.

Beginning balances.

Additions.

Sales.

Other adjustments.

Ending balance.

Long-term debt and short-term debt—calculations and disclosures.

c. Financial statement prepared during year-end audit.

From trial balance and/or auditor lead sheets.

Prepare the financial statements.

Reformat financial statements based on auditor adjustments.

Trial balances prepared by company and columns for adjusting entries. Throughout audit immediate understanding of impact of adjusting entries.

Tax provision calculations almost set automatically and net income known.

Setting of materiality for adjusting entries monitored throughout process.

Footnotes with financial statements.

Graph of key financial ratios.

d. Keep track of the hours on the job and derive client's bill from hours, multiplied by auditor hourly bill rate.

e. Comparative analysis for quarterly or other reviews made easier.

Future years analysis easier based on previous year's electronic spreadsheets.

Based on pre-established formatting procedures automatically derive new worksheets for quarterly review.

6. Calendar, due dates, and time sheets

a. Each column in a worksheet can be a day, a week, or a month.

Put own personal calendar of important events.

Have separate file for each person in a department.

Set up the calendar system using the same row and column structure for each person.

Determine people conflicts by loading each person's spreadsheet onto one screen for a number of people. Determine staff conflicts for a job, trip, or meeting very easily this way.

Assistants or secretaries could maintain these, then someone else could determine when there is a conflict.

Determine locations for individuals.

b. Due dates.

Using spreadsheet database features

SEC report filing dates.

Tax return filing dates.

Department reporting dates to management.

Personnel review dates—listing people.

Audit workpaper dates.

Quarterly reports and annual shareholders' report dates.

Insurance policy expiration dates listing:

Specific policy.

Policy number.

Agent.

Insurance company.

Special company project dates.

c. Time sheets showing hours and jobs could be performed using an electronic spreadsheet. With job cost requirements, financial amounts analysis can be performed faster. Rebilling to clients is faster and easier. Analysis of employees utilization, downtime for training, and others analyzed. Do a consolidation for payroll purposes overlaying one spreadsheet on top of a similar one.

7. Cash flow and funds statement analysis

a. Derive a cash flow statement automatically from preestablished balance sheet and profit and loss statement

b. Analyze cash sales, accounts receivable collections, accounts payable payment history, notes payment schedules, and other factors.

c. Analysis of specific factors.

Receivable—collection timing and bad debts.

Inventory turnovers and write-offs.

Accounts payable—detail and history for specific accounts.

Long-term capital debt needs.

Corporate obligations—interest debt and dividends.

Product return history.

Tax payments and collections whether local, state, federal, or foreign.

d. Money management including:

Portfolio management.

Tracking foreign currency rates.

Translation of companies' own foreign assets.

Debt servicing.

Long-term and short-term debt analysis and calculation of accrued interest, especially if based on the prime rate.

Computation of current portion of long-term debt.

e. Extrapolation of interest income.

f. Extrapolation of interest expense.

g. If used as a simple recording device for cash receipts and cash disbursements, enter automatically receipts or disbursements to maintain an automatic cash account balance analysis.

8. Record keeping simply performed

a. Spreadsheets can act as a very simple accounting record-keeping tool.

General ledger—as a summary of checking account or very limited chart of accounts requirements.

Accounts receivable—using specific amount of blocks for each customer, accounts receivable records can be set up. Certainly it is not a full accounts receivable system, but it is quite effective for a very limited number of cases. By using the block references ability and GOTO, the data can be summarized in practically any user format and generate any user report. By moving amounts to date columns based on the invoice date, an aging report can be set up.

Inventory—when a limited amount of high-priced items are being tracked.

Accounts payable—performed similar to accounts receivable.

b. Simple journals.

Sales journals.

Cash receipts journal with columns for specific sales.

c. Simple list manager. Makes lists of customers, employees, fixed assets, and inventory items. Many spreadsheets will also sort.

d. Simple project management.

Put dates on top of spreadsheets.

Set up each task as a row showing in what column it will start and where it will end.

Indicate people involved with specific tasks to be performed.

Cash disbursements journal with columns for specific types of expenses with a running balance column to know the total disbursements at any point in time.

e. Payroll.

Maintain employee register with automatic computations for income taxes and withholdings.

Write checks manually after calculation performed for that payroll period or special payroll.

Produce totals for payroll reports automatically calculated.

f. Fixed assets listing and computation of depreciation and updating of accumulated depreciation record-keeping.

g. Lease information and amounts for balance sheet entry.

h. Stock option recording by employee.

i. Capital stock recording.

j. Profit sharing.

k. Pension planning.

9. Tax preparation and calculation. There are specific tax return preparation software and service bureaus. However, there are many ways here for recording and calculating returns using an electronic spreadsheet.

a. Federal income tax.

1140 listing.

Combinations of subsidiary return information to create consolidated 1140.

Listing and derivation of individual detailed schedules.

Estate tax returns.

Individual returns with detail schedules.

b. State income tax returns.

Adjustments from federal tax returns.

Allocation of federal to all the various states in which business is done. A major worksheet could be prepared to analyze those state allocations based on various state requirements.

c. Foreign tax work.

d. Analysis of various tax treatments and alternatives.

e. Preparation of specific tax schedules.

f. Sales tax returns.

g. Quarterly and annual employee payroll and tax calculation returns.

h. Unemployment compensation calculation and returns.

i. 1099 analysis and listing requirements throughout the year.

j. Tax shelter analysis for funding sources.

10. Word processing, list managers, and other straightforward applications.

a. Simplistic word processing.

Use for short intracompany memos. The due date calendar suggestion can be referred to another block that has memos to various people concerning that due date.

Use for memos to employees, to the file, to outlines, and to short letters.

Type in words and print it out on a letter quality printer.

Very little word processing software editing capabilities.

Works well in formatting columnar information of numbers and words where word processors are more concerned with word manipulation of information by total document.

Integrated Spreadsheets to Accounting Applications

As stated previously, electronic spreadsheets are also being integrated with accounting software where historical or current information can be passed to an electronic spreadsheet for analysis or other reporting purposes. Again, this expands the immediate use of numbers. The relationship of amounts generated from accounting systems to create historical information and the need for these amounts for analysis purposes is becoming much greater.

However, you must close monthly books in a fast routine, so they can be used in a spreadsheet to alter or change direction. If amounts for one month come out at the end of the next, it may be three months before effective, corrective action can be taken:

One month of problems

One month waiting for information

One month to correct situation

If it is a seasonal problem, then no time may exist for corrective action.

EXAMPLES OF TIE-IN TO ACCOUNTING SOFTWARE

1. Audit worksheets (using a spreadsheet)—derived directly from historical information in accounting files.
2. Annual budgeting process—access to specific numbers from accounting software to a spreadsheet are important for creating a budget.
3. Forecasting—aided by access to actual information and easy transfer of information. Creating trend analysis, analyzing seasonality factors, and other statistical abilities using large amounts of historical information that can be automatically transferred.
4. Dunning letters—analyze accounts receivable aging, sort by certain due date, and print dunning letter on word processor.
5. Sorting of mail—create data base of customers with one field for zip code, then sort on this field.
6. Data measuring—create data base from historical information, then sort. Can derive largest customers, largest inventory items, largest vendors, or largest checks written in a month.

7. Another example is preparing a quarterly management report using an integrated office productivity tool and accounting software.
   Two million more ideas
   Spreadsheets are like a car: the car will not go anywhere unless you drive it. Turbo models of spreadsheets are available with much greater power than others. However, the simplest spreadsheet cannot go even two blocks without some idea and input from you. All the windows in the world will not help if you are looking out at a world that is not moving. Spreadsheets provide:

   Faster analysis.

   Simpler and faster workpaper preparation.

   Greater creativity.

The ideas listed in this chapter are only a sample of what can be done with an electronic spreadsheet.

Now it's up to you to apply them.

4

MODEL BUILDING

A power of the electronic spreadsheet is model building—analyzing and reanalyzing a business situation expressed numerically in spreadsheet form.

The phenomenon of model building, once the property of the sacred halls of graduate schools, has spread across large, medium, and small businesses.

The model provides the ability to change one or more numbers continuously in a complex spreadsheet and see the effect on all other amounts. What was too tedious and time-consuming is now performed simply, quickly, and with immediate written evidence.

This chapter explains 8 steps in creating a model. These steps can also be very useful in establishing any spreadsheet.

Modeling Examples

Financial health of the company and changing alternatives model.

Buy versus lease model

Fund alternatives model

- Evaluation of cost of debt structure
- Accounts receivable discounting (cost of this compared to line of credit)
- Short-term debt—line of credit
- Bond issue
- Research and development tax shelter
- Convertible long-term debt

- Common stock
- Preferred stock

Product pricing strategy model

- Reducing prices to increase volume
- Volume sales versus profit margins
- Bundling of products

New plant costs and alternative structures

Employee salary structure analysis

- Future skill hires and related costs
- Raises over the next year
- Skill alternatives and employee pay rates
- Commission structures and bonus scenarios
- Fringe benefits by category and related costs—current and in the future

SIMPLE MODEL BUILDING

A simple model can be based on price/volume or price sensitivity analysis. This models a real business situation. Cut prices; sell a lot more; make more money. In fact, this model created a basis for microsoftware pricing philosophy. It went as follows:

Do not code one custom package for one client. Code a standard software package for one specific application.

Add instructions (documentation) to run package.

Add other features and protection due to usage by individuals not directly trained.

Price package at a few hundred dollars.

Sell hundreds or thousands of the package.

Cut price.

Sell more.

Obtain more profit.

All software vendors, of course, wish it were that simple, but it isn't. A numerical model takes you only so far. Still, the exercise itself is beneficial.

People create models all the time without realizing that they do. It is a thought process that analyzes a business problem. Modeling can be very simple or quite complex. This is up to you. Just because a methodology is created, the actual usage of it does not have to be complicated. You should:

Start simple

Plan

Create a structure

Planning is essential in all areas of business. If you create a large, sloppy worksheet, it will be difficult for other people to follow and more likely to cause errors.

Model building is like programming, creating a standard structure and set of numbers that are to be used over and over. Don't be like the programmer who was too busy programming and had no time to design. It is okay if you are just playing around to learn how to do it. However, if a decision is based on the model, more care should be taken.

INCREASE POWER

Two methods in creating models that substantially increase the power and ease the process are:

1. Using interrelationships

USING INTERRELATIONSHIPS MEANS basing one number in the model on another. These can be based on percentages of another or some other criteria.

Example of financial projection estimate:

Cost of salaries	50 percent of sales
Bad debts	5 percent of sales
Advertising	10 percent of sales

Therefore, when one key number (sales) is changed, many other assumptions are recalculated. There is no need to enter many numbers manually after changing key number.

2. Creating submodels

CREATING SUBMODELS MEANS creating a structure. They are just smaller parts of a model and can be used to split a larger model into logical parts. For example, there could be submodels for each of a company's three divisions. Then, special factors for each division could be utilized and smaller, more controllable units created.

THE MODEL BUILDING PROCESS

Model building should take a logical process.

Figure 4–1 shows eight steps in building a model or any structural spreadsheet. Planning is a key factor.

1. Purpose
2. Details
3. Data
4. Preparation
5. Reports
6. Validation
7. What If?
8. Assessment of Results

1. Purpose.	Generally what is to be shown and to be analyzed.
2. Details.	Define exactly what is to be analyzed and to be determined.
3. Data.	Indicate exactly what data is to be used in the analysis.
4. Preparation.	Prepare the model and submodels.
5. Reports.	Print out the various reports.
6. Validation.	Review the reports to determine if calculations and other details were handled properly
7. What If?	Change key factors to determine effect on results. Possibly create other models based on: 1. Optimistic 2. Probable 3. Pessimistic
8. Assessment.	Review results and determination of any conclusions or results.

Figure 4–1 Possible steps to model building

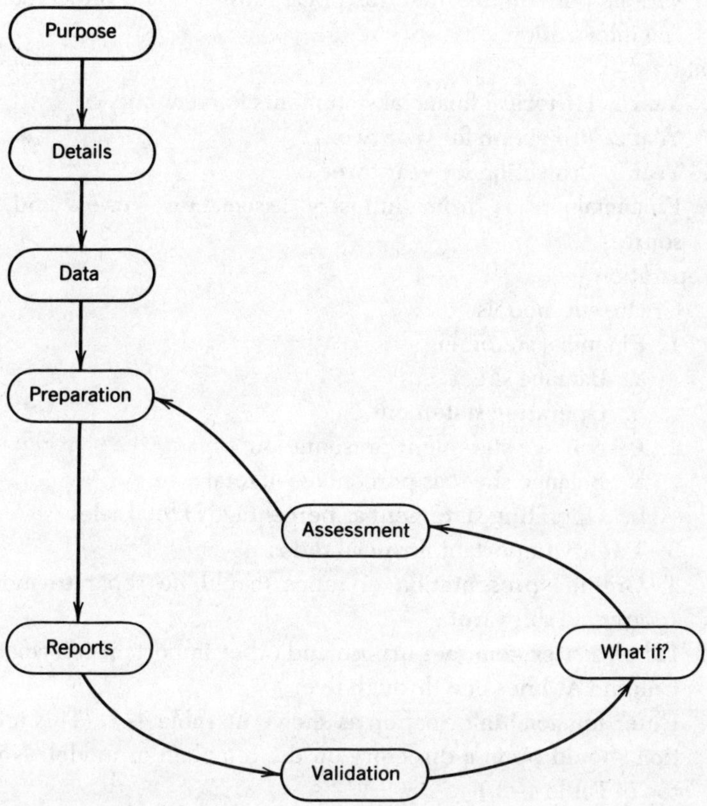

FIGURE 4–2 How To Set Up A Model: The Revolving Assessment of Model Results

MODEL BUILDING EXAMPLE

I. Purpose
   A. Provide financial review of company
   B. Provide model to look at the financial status of company
   C. Determine what areas need improvement and how they can be improved over the next several years.

II. Details
   A. Quantify purpose—calculate numerous financial ratios and compare to industry standards.
   B. Determine effects on balance sheet and operating statements of

various possibilities. Use historical, current, and projected financial information.

III. Data
  A. Year 1. Historical financial statements for year one.
  B. Year 2. Projection for year two.
  C. Year 3. Projection for year three.
  D. Financial ratios from industry association survey and other sources.

IV. Preparation
  A. Create submodels
    1. Financial statements
      a. Balance sheet
      b. Operating statement
    2. Percentage statement presentation
      a. Balance sheet as percentage of total assets
      b. Operating statement as percentage of total sales
    3. Twenty important financial ratios
    4. Graphic presentation of ratios (could be separate model in graphic software)
  B. Label. Enter general purpose and other important information in Column A, lines one through five.
  C. Enter financial information as shown in Table 4–1. (This information should be in a directory on the template or model. Note the top of Table 4–2.)
  D. Always backup files.

Column	*Row*	Statement
1. A-D	1–59	Balance Sheet (see Table 4–2)
2. F-I	1–49	Statement of Operations (see Table 4–3)
3. F-I	52–65	Selected Statistical Data (see Table 4–4)
4. A-E	67–158	Key Financial Ratios (see Table 4–5)
5. A-D	160–218	Balance Sheet in Percentages (see Table 4–6)
6. F-I	160–208	Statement of Operations in Percentages (see Table 4–7)

Tables 4–8 through 4–12 are the templates or models of the above Statements and Ratios.

Saving. Save each model in a separate file under its own model name.

E. Other instructions. Show assumptions; document model (see Tables 4–8 through 4–12 for formula documentation.

V. Reports

Print reports

A. Financial results
B. Formulas used in model
C. With or without borders (borders may be row and column)

VI. Validation

A. Review results for reasonableness and accuracy.
B. Review formulas for corrections.
C. Determine if formulas are the most meaningful in this situation.
D. Reprint reports if necessary.

VII. What if?

A. In year three, increase and decrease sales by 10 percent
B. Increase and decrease cost of goods sold by five percent
C. In year three new machine purchased for $2 million
D. ABC company acquired under purchase method and then by merger

These and many, many more can be done.

VIII. Assessment

A. Determine where the company is financially weak and where it is strong. Compare financial ratios to industry standards, and determine the trend of this company.
B. Rerun with more What Ifs, depending on observations such as:
   1. Ratio employees to sales low
   2. Net income unsatisfactory
   3. Debt/equity ratio not satisfactory
   4. What to do:
      (a) Suggest strategies
      (b) Make decisions and take action
      (c) Postpone
      (d) Further study
C. Rerun steps if useful

   Preparation (Step IV)

   Reports (Step V)

Validation (Step VI)
What if? (Step VII)

D. Review why the problem exists (this certainly can be very simple or very complex)
E. Maintain model and track future actions

SHOWING FINANCIAL ANALYSIS

The Model

The electronic spreadsheet can store this information and build on it to create additionally sophisticated models. Following is how the information appears on the screen and the formulas behind the results. The formulas used are in Lotus 1-2-3.

The financial analysis is prepared based on the company's balance sheet and operating statement. It includes input of actual results for one year and projected results for the next two years.

The Software

Dollar signs, commas between numbers, and other displays are available in many of the software packages and do not need to be typed in each time. Of course, this and other factors do vary in different types of software.

The following tables set forth the spreadsheets for the model.

TABLE 4–1 Original Financial Statements

	Table for Spreadsheet	Table showing formulas for spreadsheet
Balance sheet	4-2	4-8
Operating Statement	4-3	4-9
Selected Material Data	4-4	—
Key Financial Ratios	4-5	4-10
Balance Sheet Percentages	4-6	4-11
Operating Statement in Percentages	4-7	4-12

TABLE 4–1 Continued

Spreadsheet Company
Balance Sheet
1988 (est.), December 31, 1987 (est.), 1986
(000s Omitted)

	1988 Projected	1987 Projected	1986 Actual
Assets			
Current Assets:			
Cash	1500	800	300
Accounts receivable	4100	3100	2100
Inventory	4500	4000	3100
Prepaid expense	1500	1100	1200
Total current assets	11600	9000	6700
Property, plant and equipment			
Less: Accuumulated Depr	7800	6200	5100
Goodwill	500	500	500
Deposits	350	560	800
Other noncurrent assets	750	740	925
Total assets	21000	17000	14025
Liabilities and Shareholders' Equity			
Current liabilities			
Accounts payable	3200	1900	1200
Notes payable	500	1220	1175
Current portion of long-term debt	750	1050	1650
Accrued salaries	450	300	200
Accrued interest	200	200	175
Accrued product warranty	1200	750	600
Other liabilities	550	350	100
Total current liabilities	6850	5770	5100
Long-term debt			
Less current portion	1500	2130	2600
Other noncurrent liabilitics	600	600	125
Shareholders' Equity			
Common stock	50	50	50
Paid-in capital	2100	2100	2100
Retained earnings	9900	6350	4050
Total shareholders' equity	12050	8500	6200
Total liabilities and shareholders' equity	21000	17000	14025

TABLE 4–1 Continued

Spreadsheet Company
Statement of operations
for the year ended December 31, 1988(est.), 1987(est.), 1986
(000s Omitted)

	1988 Projected	1987 Projected	1986 Actual
Sales			
Product A	8500	5750	1800
Product B	4500	4000	6000
Product C	9000	8000	5700
Other	3000	2250	1000
Total sales	25000	20000	14500
Cost of goods sold	11400	10000	8400
Gross profit	13600	10000	6100
Selling expenses			
Advertising	750	650	500
Salaries and commissions	1750	1450	1100
Travel and entertainment	650	500	300
Other	400	200	100
Total selling expenses	3550	2800	2000
General and administrative expenses	3400	2800	2100
Operating income	6650	4400	2000
Interest expense	600	500	500
Other expense	500	600	50
Income before taxes	5550	3300	1450
Provision for income tax	2000	1000	400
Net Income	3550	2300	1050

TABLE 4–2

1	**SPREADSHEET COMPANY**			
2	**ANALYSIS OF COMPANY FINANCIALS**			
3	**BALANCE SHEET**			
4	**DECEMBER 31, 1986, 1987(est.), 1988(est.)**			
5			(000s Omitted)	
6	A	B	C	D
7		1988	1987	1986
8	ASSETS	PROJECTED	PROJECTED	ACTUAL
9	CURRENT ASSETS:			
10	CASH	1500	800	300
11	ACCOUNTS RECEIV	4100	3100	2100
12	INVENTORY	4500	4000	3100
13	PREPAID EXPENSE	1500	1100	1200
14				
15	TOTAL CURRENT ASSETS	11,600	9000	6700
16				
17	PROPERTY, PLANT & EQUIP			
18	LESS: ACCUM DEPR	7800	6200	5100
19				
20	GOODWILL	500	500	500
21	DEPOSITS	350	560	800
22	OTHER NONCUR ASSETS	750	740	925
23				
24	TOTAL ASSETS	21,000	17,000	14,025
25				
26				
27	LIABILITIES AND			
28	SHAREHOLDERS' EQ			
29				
30	CURRENT LIABILITIES			
31	ACCOUNTS PAYABLE	3200	1900	1200
32	NOTES PAYABLE	500	1220	1175
33	CURRENT PORTION OF			
34	LONG-TERM DEBT	750	1050	1650
35	ACCRUED SALARIES	450	300	200
36	ACCRUED INTEREST	200	200	175
37	ACCRUED PROD WAR	1200	750	600
38	OTHER LIABILITIES	550	350	100
39				
40				
41	TOTAL CURRENT LIABILI	6850	5770	5100
42				
43	LONG-TERM DEBT			

TABLE 4–2 Continued

		1988 PROJECTED	1987 PROJECTED	1986 ACTUAL
44	LESS CURRENT POR	1500	2130	2600
45				
46	OTHER NONCURRENT LIAB	600	600	125
47				
48	SHAREHOLDERS' EQUITY			
49	COMMON STOCK	50	50	50
50	PAID-IN CAPITAL	2100	2100	2100
51	RETAINED EARNINGS	9900	6350	4050
52				
53	TOTAL SHARE EQUITY	12,050	8500	6200
54				
55	TOTAL LIABILITIES &			
56	SHAREHOLDERS' EQUITY	21,000	17,000	14,025
57				

TABLE 4–3

	F	G	H	I
1	**SPREADSHEET COMPANY**			
2	**STATEMENT OF OPERATIONS**			
3	**FOR THE YEAR ENDED DECEMBER 31, 1988(est.), 1987(est.), 1986**			
4				
5				
6		(000s OMITTED)		
7				
8		1988	1987	1986
9		PROJECTED	PROJECTED	ACTUAL
10				
11	SALES			
12	PRODUCT A	8500	5750	1800
13	PRODUCT B	4500	4000	6000
14	PRODUCT C	9000	8000	5700
15	OTHER	3000	2250	1000
16				
17	TOTAL SALES	25,000	20,000	14,500
18				
19				
20	COST OF GOODS SOLD	11,400	10,000	8400
21				
22	GROSS PROFIT	13,600	10,000	6100
23				
24				
25	SELLING EXPENSES			
26	ADVERTISING	750	650	500
27	SALARIES & COMMI	1750	1450	1100
28	TRAVEL & ENT	650	500	300
29	OTHER SELL	400	200	100
30				
31	TOTAL MARKETING EX	3550	2800	2000
32				
33				
34	GENERAL & ADMINIS EX	3400	2800	2100
35				
36	OPERATING INCOME	6650	4400	2000
38				
39	INTEREST EXPENSE	600	500	500
40				
41	OTHER EXPENSE	500	600	50
42				
43	INCOME BEFORE TAXES	5550	3300	1450
44				

TABLE 4–3 Continued

	1988 PROJECTED	1987 PROJECTED	1986 ACTUAL
45 PROVISIONS FOR INC TAX	2000	1000	400
46			
47			
48 NET INCOME	3550	2300	1050
49			

TABLE 4–4

52	SPREADSHEET COMPANY			
53	SELECTED STATISTICAL DATA IN 000'S			
54	F	G	H	I
55		1988	1987	1986
56		PROJECTED	PROJECTED	ACTUAL
57	1. SQUARE FEET OF SPACE	80	60	30
58				
59	2. UNIT SALES PER PROD			
60	PRODUCT A	25	15	11.2
61	PRODUCT B	32	25	20
62	PRODUCT C	15	12	10
63	OTHER	18	15	12
64				
65	3. AVERAGE NUMBER OF EMPLOYEES	325	250	160

TABLE 4–5

	A	B	C	D	E
67	SPREADSHEET COMPANY				
68	KEY FINANCIAL RATIOS				
69	FOR DECEMBER 31, 1988(est.), 1987(est.), 1986				
70	and the years then ended				
71	WITH INDUSTRY STANDARDS FOR 1986				
72					
73					
74		1988	1987	1986	1986
75		PROJECTED	PROJECTED	ACTUAL	INDUSTRY
76					STANDARD
77					
78	1. CURRENT RATIO	1.69	1.56	1.31	1.54
79	Current Assets/Current Liab				
80					
81	2. QUICK or ACID TEST RATIO	0.82	0.68	0.47	0.72
82	Current Assets less Inventory				
83	and Prepaid Items/Current				
84	Liabilities				
85					
86					
87	3. INVENTORY TURNOVER	2.68	2.82	2.71	2.91
88	(Cost of Goods Sold/Average				
89	Inventory)				
90					
91	4. NET SALES TO INVENTORY	5.88	5.63	4.68	5.55
92	(Net Sales/Average Inventory)				
93					

5. AVERAGE COLLECTION PE (365* Average Accts. Rec./ Annual Credit Sales)	52.56	47.45	52.86	51.34
6. PAYMENT PERIOD FOR A/P (365* Average Accts. Pay./ Annual Credit Purchases)	85.39	62.17	60.00	78.66
7. DEBT TO EQUITY (Debt/Shareholders' Equity)	0.74	1.00	1.26	0.95
8. RETURN ON SHAREHOLDRS' EQ (Net Income/Average Shareholders' Equity)	0.35	0.31	0.17	0.39
9. RETURN ON TOTAL ASSETS (Net Income/Average Total Assets)	0.19	0.15	0.08	0.25
10. EFFECTIVE TAX RATE (Income Tax/Income before Taxes)	0.36	0.30	0.28	0.34
11. OPERATING INCOME TO INTEREST EXPENSE (Operating Income/Int. Exp.)	5.92	4.60	2.10	5.67
12. SALES TO WORKING CAPITAL (Sales/Working Capital)	5.26	6.19	9.06	5.11

TABLE 4–5 Continued

		1988 PROJECTED	1987 PROJECTED	1986 ACTUAL	1986 INDUSTRY STANDARD
124	13. SALES PER SQUARE FOOT	0.31	0.33	0.48	0.37
125	(Sales/Average Square Feet)				
126					
127	14. SALES PER SELL. PAYROLL	14.29	13.79	13.18	15.36
128	(Sales/Total Selling				
129	Salaries and Commiss)				
130					
131	15. SALES PER AVERAGE NUMBER	76.92	80.00	90.63	78.88
132	OF EMPLOYEES				
133	(Sales/Avg No. of Employees)				
134					
135	16. AVERAGE SALES PRICE PER				
136	UNIT SOLD				
137	PRODUCT A	340	380	160	n/a
138	PRODUCT B	140	160	300	n/a
139	PRODUCT C	600	670	570	n/a
140	(Sales/units per product				
141	sold)				
142					
143	17. AVERAGE COST OF GOODS				
144	SOLD PER UNIT SOLD	130	150	160	n/a
145	(Cost of Goods Sold/Total				
146	Units Sold)				
147					

18. INCREASE IN SALES (Sales Current Year − Sales Previous Year/Sales Prev Yr)	0.25	0.38	N/A		n/a
19. INCREASE IN GROSS MARGIN (Gross Margin Current Year − G M Prev Year/G M Prev Yr)	0.36	0.64	N/A	n/a	
20. INCREASE IN NET INCOME (Net Income Current Year − Net Income Prev Yr/N I)	0.51	1.20	N/A	n/a	

Note: Above are examples only, always check computations

TABLE 4–6

	A	B	C	D
160	SPREADSHEET COMPANY			
161	ANALYSIS OF COMPANY FINANCIALS			
162	BALANCE SHEET			
163	DECEMBER 31, 1986, 1987(est.), 1988(est.)			
164	PERCENT TO TOTAL			
165				
166				
167		1988	1987	1986
168	ASSETS	PROJECTED	PROJECTED	ACTUAL
169	CURRENT ASSETS:			
170	CASH	7.14%	4.71%	2.14%
171	ACCOUNTS RECEIV	19.52%	18.24%	14.97%
172	INVENTORY	21.43%	23.53%	22.10%
173	PREPAID EXPENSE	7.14%	6.47%	8.56%
174				
175	TOTAL CURRENT AS	55.24%	52.94%	47.77%
176				
177	PROP, PLANT & EQ			
178	LESS: ACCUM DEPR	37.14%	36.47%	36.36%
179				
180	GOODWILL	2.38%	2.94%	3.57%
181	DEPOSITS	1.67%	3.29%	5.70%
182	OTHER ASSETS	3.57%	4.35%	6.60%
183				
184	TOTAL ASSETS	100.00%	100.00%	100.00%
185				
186				
187	LIABILITIES AND			
188	SHAREHOLDERS' EQUITY			
189				
190	CURRENT LIABILITIES			
191	ACCOUNTS PAYABLE	15.24%	11.18%	8.56%
192	NOTES PAYABLE	2.38%	7.18%	8.38%
193	CURRENT PORTION OF	0.00%	0.00%	0.00%
194	LONG-TERM DEBT	3.57%	6.18%	11.76%
195	ACCRUED SALARIES	2.14%	1.76%	1.43%
196	ACCRUED INTEREST	0.95%	1.18%	1.25%
197	ACCRUED PRODUCT WAR	5.71%	4.41%	4.28%
198	OTHER LIABILITIES	2.62%	2.06%	0.71%
199				
200				
201	TOTAL CURRENT LI	32.62%	33.94%	36.36%
202				

TABLE 4–6 (Continued)

		1988 PROJECTED	1987 PROJECTED	1986 ACTUAL
203	LONG-TERM DEBT			
204	LESS CURRENT POR	7.14%	12.53%	18.54%
205				
206				
207	OTHER NONCURRENT LI	2.86%	3.53%	0.89%
208				
209	SHAREHOLDERS' EQUITY			
210	COMMON STOCK	0.24%	0.29%	0.36%
211	PAID-IN CAPITAL	10.00%	12.35%	14.97%
212	RETAINED EARNINGS	47.14%	37.35%	28.88%
213				
214	TOTAL SHARE EQUITY	57.38%	50.00%	44.21%
215				
216	TOTAL LIABILITIES &			
217	SHAREHOLDERS' EQ	100.00%	100.00%	100.00%
218				

TABLE 4–7

	F	G	H	I
160	SPREADSHEET COMPANY			
161	STATEMENT OF OPERATIONS			
162	FOR THE YEARS ENDED DECEMBER 31, 1988(est.), 1987(est.), 1986			
163	AS PERCENT OF SALES			
164				
165				
166				
167		1988	1987	1986
168		PROJECTED	PROJECTED	ACTUAL
169				
170	SALES			
171	PRODUCT A	34.00%	28.75%	12.41%
172	PRODUCT B	18.00%	20.00%	41.38%
173	PRODUCT C	36.00%	40.00%	39.31%
174	OTHER	12.00%	11.25%	6.90%
175				
176	TOTAL SALES	100.00%	100.00%	100.00%
177				
178				
179	COST OF GOODS SOLD	45.60%	50.00%	57.93%
180				
181	GROSS PROFIT	54.40%	50.00%	42.07%
182				
183				
184	SELLING EXPENSES			
185	ADVERTISING	3.00%	3.25%	3.45%
186	SALARIES & COMMIS	7.00%	7.25%	7.59%
187	TRAVEL & ENTERTAIN	2.60%	2.50%	2.07%
188	OTHER	1.60%	1.00%	0.69%
189				
190	TOTAL SELLING EX	14.20%	14.00%	13.79%
191				
192				
193	GENERAL & ADMINIS EX	13.60%	14.00%	14.48%
194				
195	OPERATING INCOME	26.60%	22.00%	13.79%
196				
197				
198	INTEREST EXPENSE	2.40%	2.50%	3.45%
199				
200	OTHER EXPENSES	2.00%	3.00%	0.34%
201				
202	INCOME BEFORE TAXES	22.20%	16.50%	10.00%

TABLE 4–7 (Continued)

		1988 PROJECTED	1987 PROJECTED	1986 ACTUAL
203				
204	PROVISION FOR FED TAX	8.00%	5.00%	2.76%
205				
206				
207	NET INCOME	14.20%	11.50%	7.24%
208				

TABLE 4–8

SPREADSHEET COMPANY
ANALYSIS OF COMPANY FINANCIALS
BALANCE SHEET
DECEMBER 31, 1986, 1987(est.), 1988(est.)

	(000s OMITTED)		
ASSETS	1988 PROJECTED	1987 PROJECTED	1986 ACTUAL
CURRENT ASSETS:			
CASH	1500	800	300
ACCOUNTS REC	4100	3100	2100
INVENTORY	4500	4000	3100
PREPAID EXPENSE	1500	1100	1200
TOTAL CURRENT ASSETS	@SUM(B10..B14)	@SUM(C10..C14)	@SUM(D10..D14)
PROPERTY, PLANT & EQUIP			
LESS: ACCUM DEPR	7800	6200	5100
GOODWILL	500	500	500
DEPOSITS	350	560	800
OTHER NONCURRENT ASSETS	750	740	925
TOTAL ASSETS	@SUM(B15..B23)	@SUM(C15..C23)	@SUM(D15..D23)

LIABILITIES AND SHAREHOLDERS' EQUITY			
CURRENT LIABILITIES			
ACCOUNTS PAYABLE	3200	1900	1200
NOTES PAYABLE	500	1220	1175
CURRENT PORTION OF LONG-TERM DEBT	750	1050	1650
ACCRUED SALARIES	450	300	200
ACCRUED INTEREST	200	200	175
ACCRUED PRODUCT WARRANTY	1200	750	600
OTHER LIABILITIES	550	350	100
TOTAL CURRENT LIABILITIES	@SUM(B31..B39)	@SUM(C31..C39)	@SUM(D31..D39)
LONG-TERM DEBT LESS CURRENT PORTION	1500	2130	2600
OTHER NONCURRENT LIABILITIES	600	600	125
SHAREHOLDERS' EQUITY			
COMMON STOCK	50	50	50
PAID-IN CAPITAL	2100	2100	2100
RETAINED EARNINGS	9900	6350	4050
TOTAL SHAREHOLDERS' EQUITY	@SUM(B49..B52)	@SUM(C49..C52)	@SUM(D49..D52)
TOTAL LIABILITIES & SHAREHOLDERS' EQUITY	+B41+B44+B46+B53	+C41+C44+C46+C53	+D41+D44+D46+D53

TABLE 4–9

SPREADSHEET COMPANY
STATEMENT OF OPERATIONS
FOR THE YEAR ENDED DECEMBER 31, 1988(est.), 1987(est.), 1986
(000s OMITTED)

	1988 PROJECTED	1987 PROJECTED	1986 ACTUAL
SALES			
PRODUCT A	8500	5750	1800
PRODUCT B	4500	4000	6000
PRODUCT C	9000	8000	5700
OTHER	3000	2250	1000
TOTAL SALES	@SUM(G12..G15)	@SUM(H12..H15)	@SUM(I12..I15)
COST OF GOODS SOLD	11,400	10,000	8400
GROSS PROFIT	+G17-G20	+H17-H20	+I17-I20
SELLING EXPENSES			
ADVERTISING	750	650	500
SALARIES & COMMISSIONS	1750	1450	1100
TRAVEL & ENTERTAINMENT	650	500	300
OTHER	400	200	100
TOTAL SELLING EXPENSE	@SUM(G26..G29)	@SUM(H26..H29)	@SUM(I26..I29)
GENERAL & ADMINIS EXPENSES	3400	2800	2100

OPERATING INCOME	+G22-G31-G34	+H22-H31-H34	+I22-I31-I34
INTEREST EXPENSE	600	500	500
OTHER EXPENSE	500	600	50
INCOME BEFORE TAXES	+G36-G39-G41	+H36-H39-H41	+I36-I39-I41
PROVISIONS FOR INC TAX	2000	1000	400
NET INCOME	+G43-G45	+H43-H45	+I43-I45

TABLE 4–10

SPREADSHEET COMPANY
KEY FINANCIAL RATIOS
FOR DECEMBER 31, 1988(est.), 1987(est.), 1986
and the years then ended
WITH INDUSTRY STANDARDS FOR 1986

	1986 PROJECTED	1987 PROJECTED	1986 ACTUAL
1. CURRENT RATIO Current Assets/Current Liab	+B15/B41	+C15/C41	+D15/D41
2. QUICK or ACID TEST RATIO Current Assets less Inventory and Prepaid Items/ Current Liabilities	(+B15-B12-B13)/B41	(+C15-C12-C13)/C41	(+D15-D12-D13)/D41
3. INVENTORY TURNOVER (Cost of Goods Sold/Aver. Inventory)	+G20/((B12+C12)/2)	+H20/((C12+D12)/2)	
4. NET SALES TO INVENTORY (Net Sales / Average Inventory)	+G17/((B12+C12)/2)	+H17/((C12+D12)/2)	
5. AVERAGE COLLECTION PERIOD 365 * Average Accts. Rec./ Annual Credit Sales	365* (((B11+C11)/2)/ G17)	+365*(((C11+D11)/2)/ H17)	365*(D11/I17)

6. PAYMENT PERIOD FOR A/P (365* Average Accts. Pay./ Annual Credit Purchases)	365*((B31+C31)/2)			
7. DEBT TO EQUITY (Debt / Shareholders' Equity)	@SUM(B41..B48)/B56	@SUM(C41..C48)/C56	@SUM(D41..D48)/D56	
8. RETURN ON SHRHLDRS' EQUITY (Net Income / Average Shareholders' Equity)	+G48/((B55+C55)/2)	+H48/((C55+D55)/2)	+I48/((D55+6000)/2)	*Assumed a 6000 beginning balance
9. RETURN ON TOTAL ASSETS (Net Income / Average Total Assets)	+G48/((B24+C24)/2)	+H48/((C24+D24)/2)	+I48/((D24+12000)/2)	*Assumed a $12,000 beginning balance
10. EFFECTIVE TAX RATE (Income Tax / Income before Taxes	+G45/G43	+H45/H43	+I45/I43	
11. OPERATING INCOME TO INTEREST EXPENSE (Operating Income / Int. Exp.)	+G36/G39	+H36/H39	+I36/I39	
12. SALES TO WORKING CAPITAL (Sales / Working Capital)	+G17/(B15-B41)	+H17/(C15-C41)	+I17/(D15-D41)	
13. SALES PER SQUARE FOOT (Sales / Average Square Feet)	+G17/G57	+H17/H57	+I17/I57	
14. SALES PER MKETING PAYROLL (Sales / Total Marketing Salaries and Commissions)	+G17/G27	+H17/H27	+I17/I27	

TABLE 4–10 Continued

	1986 PROJECTED	1987 PROJECTED	1986 ACTUAL
15. SALES PER AVERAGE NUMBER OF EMPLOYEES (Sales / Avg No. of Employees)	+G17/G65	+H17/H65	+I17/I65
16. AVERAGE SALES PRICE PER UNIT SOLD			
PRODUCT A	+G12/G60	+H12/H60	+I12/I60
PRODUCT B	+G13/G61	+H13/H61	+I13/I61
PRODUCT C	+G14/G62	+H14/H62	+I14/I62
(Sales / Units per Product Sold)			
17. AVERAGE COST OF GOODS SOLD PER UNIT SOLD (Cost of Goods Sold / Total Units Sold)	+G20/ @SUM(G60..G63)	+H20/ @SUM(H60..H63)	+I20/@SUM(I60..I63)
18. INCREASE IN SALES (Sales Current Year – Sales Previous Year / Sales Prev Yr)	(+G17-H17)/H17	(+H17-I17)/I17	N/A
19. INCREASE IN GROSS MARGIN (Gross Margin Current Year – G M PrevYear / G M Prev Yr)	(+G22-H22)/H22	(+H22/I22)/I22	N/A
20. INCREASE IN NET INCOME (Net Income Current Year – Net Income Prev Yr / N I Prev Yr)	(+G36-H36)/H36	(+H36-I36)/I36	N/A

Note: Above ratios are only examples and may require additional data not shown or different formulas. Also additional documentation is required.

TABLE 4–11

SPREADSHEET COMPANY
ANALYSIS OF COMPANY FINANCIALS
BALANCE SHEET
DECEMBER 31, 1986, 1987(est.), 1988(est.)

	(000s OMITTED)		
	1988	1987	1986
ASSETS	PROJECTED	PROJECTED	ACTUAL
CURRENT ASSET			
CASH	+B10/B24	+C10/C24	+D10/D24
ACCOUNTS RECEIVABLE	+B12/B24	+C11/C24	+D11/D24
INVENTORY	+B12/B24	+C12/C24	+D12/D24
PREPAID EXPENSE	+B13/B24	+C13/C24	+D13/D25
TOTAL CURRENT ASSETS	+B15/B24	+C15/C24	+D15/D24
PROPERTY, PLANT & EQUIP			
LESS: ACCUM DEPR	+B18/B24	+C18/C24	+D18/D24
GOODWILL	+B20/B24	+C20/C24	+D20/D24
DEPOSITS	+B21/B24	+C21/C24	+D21/D24
OTHER ASSETS	+B22/B24	+C22/C24	+D22/D24
TOTAL ASSETS	+B24/B24	C124/C24	+D24/D24
LIABILITIES AND SHAREHOLDERS' EQUITY			
CURRENT LIABILITIES			
ACCOUNTS PAYABLE	+B31/B56	+C31/C56	+D31/D56
NOTES PAYABLE	+B32/B56	+C32/C56	+D32/D56
CURRENT PORTION OF LONG-TERM DEBT	+B34/B56	+C34/C56	+D34/D56
ACCRUED SALARIES	+B35/B56	+C35/C56	+D35/C56
ACCRUED INTEREST	+B36/B56	+C36/C56	+D36/D56
ACCRUED PRODUCT WAR	+B37/B56	+C37/C56	+D37/D56
OTHER LIABILITIES	+B38/B56	+C38/C56	+D38/D56
TOTAL CURRENT LIABILI	+B41/B56	+C41/C56	+D41/D56
LONG-TERM DEBT			
LESS CURRENT PORTION	+B44/B56	+C44/B56	+D44/D56
OTHER NONCURRENT LI	+B46/B56	+C46/B56	+D46/D56
SHAREHOLDERS' EQUITY			
COMMON STOCK	+B49/B56	+C49/C56	+D49/D56
PAID-IN CAPITAL	+B50/B56	+C50/C56	+D50/D56
RETAINED EARNINGS	+B51/B56	+C51/C56	+D51/D56
TOTAL SHAREHOLDERS' EQ	+B53/B56	C53/C56	+D53/D56
TOTAL LIABILITIES & SHAREHOLDERS' EQUITY	+B56/B56	+C56/C56	+D56/D56

TABLE 4–12

SPREADSHEET COMPANY
STATEMENT OF OPERATIONS
FOR THE YEAR ENDED DECEMBER 31, 1988(est.), 1987(est.), 1986

	(000s OMITTED)		
	1988 PROJECTED	1987 PROJECTED	1986 ACTUAL
SALES			
PRODUCT A	+G12/G17	+H12/H17	+I12/I17
PRODUCT B	+G13/G17	+H13/H17	+I13/I17
PRODUCT C	+G14/G17	+H14/H17	+I14/I17
OTHER	+G15/G17	+H15/H17	+I15/I17
TOTAL SALES	+G17/G17	+H17/H17	+I17/I17
COST OF GOODS SOLD	+G20/G17	+H20/H17	+I20/I17
GROSS PROFIT	+G22/G17	+H22/H17	+I22/I17
SELLING EXPENSES			
ADVERTISING	+G26/G17	+H26/H17	+I26/I17
SALARIES & COMMISSIONS	+G27/G17	+H27/H17	+I27/H17
TRAVEL & ENTERTAIN-MENT	+G28/G17	+H28/H17	+I28/I17
OTHER	+G29/G17	+H29/H17	+I29/I17
TOTAL SELLING EX-PENSES	+G31/G17	+H31/H17	+I31/I17
GENERAL & ADMINIS EX-PENSES	+G34/G17	+H34/H17	+I34/I17
OPERATING INCOME	+G36/G17	+H36/H17	+I36/I17
INTEREST EXPENSE	+G39/G17	+H39/H17	+I39/I17
OTHER EXPENSE	+G41/G17	+H41/H17	+I41/I17
INCOME BEFORE TAXES	+G43/G17	+H43/H17	+I43/I17
PROVISIONS FOR INC TAX	+G45/G17	+H45/H17	+I45/I17
NET INCOME	+G48/G17	H48/H17	+I48/I17

TABLE 4–13

	K	L	M	
1	FINANCIAL	ANALYSIS	DIRECTORY	
2		Column	Row	
3	1.	A-D	1-59	Balance Sheet
4	2.	F-I	1-49	Statement of Operations
5	3.	F-I	52–65	Selected Statistical Data
6	4.	A-E	67–158	Key Financial Ratios
7	5.	A-D	160–218	Balance Sheet in Percentages
8	6.	F-I	160–208	Statement of Operation in
9				Percentages

Edit Checks

Edit checks can be added to the attached model, each performing a separate check on the logic and reasonableness of the results in the model.

Examples of edit checks in the attached model are:

Example 1.
Edit Check:
Balance Sheet
Total Assets = Total Liabilities + Total Shareholders' Equity
(In Table 4–2)

Lotus Formula :
IF(+B25=+B26,@ERR)

Example 2.
Edit Check:
Statement of Operations
Total Sales in a projected year will not be more than 150% of the previous year's sales.
(In Table 4–3)

Lotus Formula
1987 Projected compared to 1986
IF(+H17<I17×150%,+H17,@ERR)

Many other examples are possible. It is important to use numerous edit routines to provide some self-checking ability in the model. The first time a model is created it should be as simple as possible. In future uses a greater degree of sophistication should be built in and more of these self-checking formulas added to the model.

5

DATA BASES AND DATA BASE MANAGEMENT SYSTEMS (DBMS)

Data bases are large amounts of closely or loosely related pieces of data. The pieces of data are organized in the form of records, which are sets of data pertaining to one event or entry, and files, which are sets of related records. The most common analogy is an office filing cabinet. Picture a filing cabinet, for example, with manually prepared inventory cards. A data base record would be one item of inventory with all of the pertinent data regarding that item, and the file would be all of the inventory records. Since there may be several types of inventory, raw materials, supplies, finished units, and units-in-process, for example, there may be the need for several different files of records. The major difference between the manual filing system and the data base for inventory is that the manual system has some type of order as you open the file drawer. In other words, as you see the inventory cards, they have been filed in some sequence, either numerically or alphabetically, for ease of access. A data base of inventory items is stored in no particular order or sequence and requires computer software to make the data useful and accessible.

A DBMS is a set of computer programs (software) that enters the filing cabinet electronically, accesses one or a number of files, and performs certain user prescribed functions to give the user information that can be be used to support the decision-making process. These systems were developed originally for mainframe computer systems and have been available since the 1960s, but often programming specialists were required to write programs that could provide the needed information to the end user. Therefore, organizations that wanted to use DBMS had to invest in significant overhead costs. Microbased DBMS allows the user to build and access a data base to obtain information without the expense and delay formerly associated with accessing information using more complex mainframe and minibased systems. (Figure 5–1)

The application of a microbased DBMS is limited largely by the user's imagination. Of course, a more sophisticated DBMS allows the user the ability to design applications more complex than the less sophisticated ones. Even less sophisticated DBMS programs can be useful if the needs of the user are not very strenuous. The following case examples may be helpful:

CASE 1. Salesmen in this company handle many current and potential customers. Managing customer or client lists can be very time-consuming, and useful information is not readily available. Salesmen try to call on each client once a quarter and each potential client once each six months. Promotional sales are often used but only large clients would benefit; they can buy in the quantity needed to benefit from special promotions.

For example, simple DBMS would be helpful if a salesman wishes to list the clients who have not been visited or called in the last three or six months for purposes of keeping in touch or follow-up. Salesmen can also keep current mailing lists indexed by company size, type, and geographic location code for the direct mailings. The mailing list application can also be used to sort addresses according to zip code, city, and state either for bulk mailing or direct mail. A further application can include the printing of mailing labels from a DBMS print routine.

CASE 2. This company's corporate telephone book was never up to date because of internal growth, acquisition of subsidiaries, and the resultant change in personnel. The cost of updating and printing became prohibitive given the numerous times it was necessary. Therefore, the corporate telephone book was converted to a DBMS. A complete, current directory comes out each month in the form of a diskette which is copied and sent to 45 departments. Hard (paper) copies are printed only at the department head's discretion and photocopies are distributed within departments. Some departments opted to keep the company telephone numbers and addresses on magnetic media only,

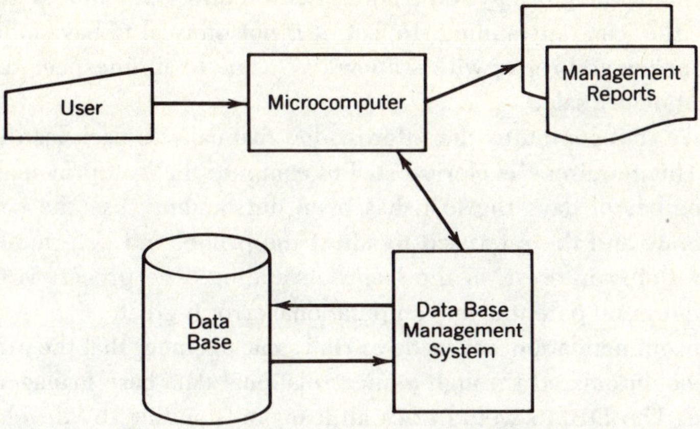

FIGURE 5–1 Data Base Management, The CPU, and The User

rather than print a company telephone directory. Moreover, any department wishing to send information to all, a few, or a specific segment of employees has the ability to print mailing labels for internal distribution or routing.

These two cases show relatively simple uses for DBMS, but they are significant in that the data base can be updated with ease and it meets the needs of the user. Moreover, electronic spreadsheets could not provide the same functional assistance that the DBMS does in these situations.

More complex applications of the DBMS's power may be limited only by one's imagination. Another case example will help.

CASE 3. Hall Mortgage makes loans to residential and commercial developers. Interest is paid monthly and when the property is sold, the developer will pay off the loan. Loan rates vary with the assessed risk of the developer, but all are based on the prime rate with a percentage added. Interest is computed in a daily basis on the unpaid balance. Developers may have several developments underway or have developments that progress over several months. Therefore, it may be necessary to borrow at intervals, which means that the rate may differ for each amount borrowed, depending on the prime rate's movement.

Also, the developer may sell a portion of the development and pay off part of the loan outstanding. In fact, it is not unusual to have a developer borrow and repay within a few days, due to an unexpected consummation of a sale.

Hall's staff computes the interest due manually as each loan is repaid. This requires the clerical staff to compute the loan principal and the number of days the loan has been outstanding, use the correct prime rate and the rate used to adjust the prime, and determine the correct dollar interest on the loan outstanding. The process is time-consuming and potential for computational error is great.

A recommendation was made to Hall's management that the process could be automated through a microrelational data base management system. The DBMS would track all loans outstanding, by developer, and the appropriate prime rate for each loan and interest rate adjustment. Further, the DBMS would compute the amount of interest accrued on each loan for purposes of loan repayment receipts and for financial statements to determine the accrued interest receivable asset. Finally, the DBMS would have a routine which would print invoices in Hall's forms and print hard copies of each borrower's activity for the year.

The relationship between the various files is shown in Figure 5–2. The files are related by a record index. In the first file the borrower tables is indexed to the loan table through the client number. Therefore, when a developer obtains a new loan there is no need to reenter information on the borrower table but only to enter the information on the loan table. The loan table is indexed to the prime rate table and the prime rate adjustment table through the interest rate on the loan table. The interest rate on the loan table could be a letter or number code which ties to the other two tables.

Deciding which DBMS to buy is dependent on a needs analysis. That is, what do you need the package to do now? An equally important question is what will you need the package to do in the future? Buying for present needs is always risky because first uses are often elementary, until a zone of user comfort develops and then other uses are thought of. As in most purchase decisions, the key to success is planning.

In the planning process, if a purchase is made simply to get an understanding of what DBMS is all about, or for simple applications, then a low-priced program such as PFS:File™ or PFS:First Choice™ is good. When a major

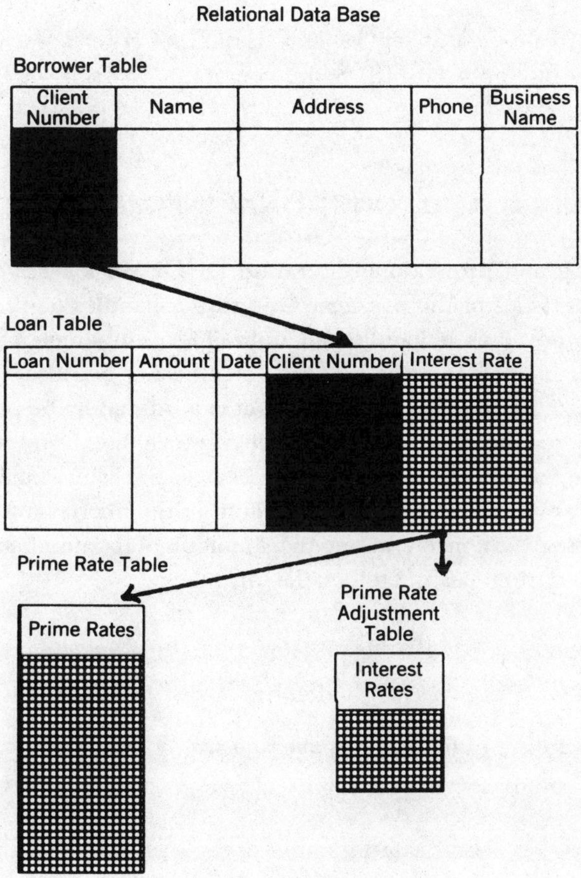

FIGURE 5–2 Relational Data Base

application is to be made using the interaction of several files, a more sophisticated DBMS like dBaseIII, Knowledge Man, and RBase 5000 should be considered.

Do not forget that what one DBMS can do, others may not, or may not do as well. Consider things that you may want to do but have always done manually. Graphic analysis, for example, may never have been an important need because of the cost and technical abilities required. Using certain DBMS packages can give the user easy access to valuable graphic aids. Therefore, consider what you would like rather than duplicating the manual process you now have.

The DBMS Evaluation Sheet (Table 5–1) outlines criteria the user should consider before buying a DBMS. Some comments to each section may be helpful.

GENERAL AND FUNCTIONAL INFORMATION

Most advertising and promotional literature for DBMS focuses on the numerical characteristics of the package. One says it handles one million records while another says it handles an unlimited number of records. The number of records handled is really of little significance because disk space is the outer limit to the number of records that can ultimately be processed at one time. The real question is how efficiently can the DBMS process a selected number of records. Often information on program efficiency is not published except in software evaluations found in the microcomputer press. If record accessing is a consideration, an estimation of the number of records that can be stored can be estimated by the formula:

Size of the magnetic storage device

divided by

Number of fields times average size of each field

yields

Estimated number of records

So that a system with a 10-megabyte hard disk having an average record size of 15 fields with an average field size of 25 characters would yield:

10,000,000

divided by

15 times 25

yields

26,000 records

Having a Julian calendar (days since a base date such as 01/01/01) may be of little significance to some users, but is of paramount importance to companies with applications like the previously mentioned Hall Mortgage case.

TABLE 5–1
DBMS EVALUATION SHEET

I. General and functional information
- Name of program: ___________.
- Level of sophistication: (list manager, relational data base, etc.)
- Maximum number of fields in each record:
- Maximum field length: Memo field available: Maximum memo field length:
- Maximum records handled:
- Maximum record length:
- Maximum number of variables:
- Mathematical functions: (internal Julian calendar, Q−,*,/,other)
- Multiple floppies can be used to store data base:

II. Friendliness and accessibility of software support
- Tutorial disk:
- Tutorial routine in documentation:
- Reference card:
- Quick manual: (key elements of the documentation in a reference guide)
- Examples provided in documentation:
- User support:
  - Hotline available during working hours
  - Hotline available 24 hours each day
  - Hotline an 800 telephone number

III. Necessary hardware configuration
- Operating system required: (may be more than one)
- Minimum RAM necessary:
- CPU compatibility: (e.g. IBM–PC, XT, or AT)
- Peripheral support:
  - Graphics card
  - Hard disk (e.g. can program reside on hard disk, can data and program reside on hard disk, program resides on hard disk with floppy in another disk drive, other combinations)
  - Printer(s)
  - Mouse
  - Plotters (if software has graphics abilities)

IV. Interaction with user
- Menu driven:
- Command driven: Menu and command driven: (user choice)
- Help screens:
- Can be programmed to perform automated applications:
- Security protected by password or hardware interface:
- Programs written and available from other sources to apply the DBMS:

V. Data sharing with other programs
- Shares data with:
  - Files and programs created only by the DBMS itself
  - 1-2-3

TABLE 5–1 Continued

dBase II
dBase III™
PFS:File™
ASCII files™
Others: (RBase V™, Knowledge Man™, etc.)

VI. Major functional uses
   A. Searches _____ maximum criteria simultaneously
   B. Sorts _______ maximum criteria simultaneously
   C. Search logic: AND; OR; NOT; IF . . . THEN; IF . . . THEN . . . ELSE; OTHER
   D. Search criteria: YES/NO; DATE; DOLLAR; FLOATING POINT; INTERGER; STRING; OTHER
   E. Search is upper/lower case dependant: Search is not upper/lower case dependent: Upper/lower case dependence defined by user:
   F. Search allows wild card: Search allows "sounds like" or "looks like":

VII. Output capabilities
   A. On-screen form design capability
   B. Form design screens
   C. Response checking (disallows certain input from being made, e.g., letters where date should be)
   D. Range checking (disallows certain data from being input if it exceeds a range)
   E. Print to forms: (invoices, mailing labels, etc.)
   F. Graphics abilities: (none, bar, pie, stacked bar, line)

VIII. Other considerations
   A. Published evaluations
   B. Recommendations of other users
   C. Actual hands-on use *

Hands-on use is recommended. However, due to different data management needs performance criteria is impossible to evaluate via a check sheet. One should see the DBMS in operation using actual data preferably at a reference user's site rather than the vendor's. Ask the vendor for a "loaner" or an evaluation copy. If multiple copy purchases are at stake, the vendor may be very willing to provide the service.

FRIENDLINESS AND ACCESSIBILITY OF SOFTWARE SUPPORT

Having tutorial help, either in the form of cases, suggested applications, a tutorial disk, a tutorial section in the user manual, interactive video-disk or a combination of these is a must. Reference cards or quick manuals are benefits (see chapter on hints and tips). Since DBMS is more difficult to master than other types of software, some form of user support is mandatory. Vendor support becomes much more important.

NECESSARY HARDWARE CONFIGURATION

There is nothing more discouraging than to make your plans, make your purchase, and then get to the office only to find that the program needs 384 Kb RAM and you have only 256 Kb. Make sure your computer configuration meets the needs of the DBMS.

INTERACTION WITH THE USER

Some people are persuaded that a menu driven program is better or easier to use than a command driven program. A menu driven program has choices that can be selected by letter or by cursor movement, while command driven programs may have nothing more on the screen than a dot in the upper left-hand corner. Initially, a menu driven program may seem easier to use, but once the user becomes accustomed to the command language, the menu becomes an irritant. More important is how well the documentation is written and how comprehensive and helpful the tutorial is.

DATA SHARING WITH OTHER PROGRAMS

The power of DBMS can be increased substantially by having the ability to share data with other software packages. For example, if one is not sure whether a particular DBMS will be suitable for the long run, one way to hedge the choice is to make sure that records created under one DBMS can be transported to another DBMS. This ability prevents having to reinput the data manually if another more sophisticated package is developed or demanded.

MAJOR FUNCTIONAL USES

Remember, the greatest use of a DBMS is finding, retrieving, and using stored data. Therefore, functions such as searches will be a part of every DBMS. The application of the search function may be in the form of FIND (criteria 1), and (criteria 2), and (criteria 3), and . . . .

> For example, FIND all clients with the last name Jones who live in the Southeast Region, live in a Standard Metropolitan Area, have purchased less than $500, and made their last purchase in 1984.

The illustration demonstrates the significance of search criteria and why it would be important to know how many criteria the DBMS can use simultaneously.

The search function should allow the user to define the search criteria in upper case, lower case, and either upper or lower case. For example, a search for the word *base* may find only base, not Base or BASE. The user should be able to define the search criteria in a manner such that the information needed is obtained whether it is in upper, lower, or a combination of both.

OUTPUT CAPABILITIES

A very valuable feature is to have on-screen viewing of the form design before hard copy output. This is particularly important for the organization wishing to have output to company-specific forms such as invoices, purchase orders, or company-designed forms.

OTHER CONSIDERATIONS

Depending on the number of copies of the software the organization is considering buying, the availability of licensing agreements and corporate purchases of software should be investigated with software developers.

There is a hidden cost associated with any software package: The time it takes to learn the program's intricacies, syntax, and command language. This cost is often greater with a DBMS program than with any other software because of the general unfamiliarity of the user with data base concepts and the potential power of the software. It may take a few hours, a few days, or even a few weeks to learn a DBMS, depending on the complexity of the program and the degree of skill the user desires to obtain. Many users will obtain the services of a micro data base consultant to suggest the system and the DBMS package, and to set up the applications. In this situation, the cost is out of pocket rather than hidden. Whether one goes it alone or hires the services of an expert to help with the purchase, the hardware and software are only a part of the cost.

The use of DBMS is certainly not as simple as spreadsheet usage. There are many more user, design, and application considerations.

Finally, the cost of inputting the data into the data base should be considered. Once the format for the data records has been set, the input can be done by a clerical worker, but it is a cost that should not be overlooked.

Remember, a DBMS has these four advantages over a manual system:

Current Information

Compactness

Speed

Less Clerical Work

6

MANAGER'S GUIDE TO WORD PROCESSING

Any guidebook to microcomputer software must discuss a very frequently used type of microcomputer software—word processing. While electronic spreadsheets move the business decision support systems, word processing software is the workhorse of all microcomputer use. Word processing began with dedicated computer hardware and software; that is, earlier word processing systems could do nothing else but process words. The technology of word processing changed the secretary's role like no other technology since the typewriter and telephone were first placed into offices.

Basically, a word processing system is a computer system that allows the user to type manuscripts, letters, documents, and other kinds of written matter while viewing the results on a CRT screen. The user can store the document on magnetic media for further revision later or produce a paper copy immediately. However, this feature is just the beginning. There are many other features that make word processing almost a necessity to an efficient and effective office environment.

Some systems have a CRT screen that is larger than the normal microcomputer screen so one whole page can be displayed at a time.

There are several examples that can serve to show the power and usefulness of word processing. As a manuscript is being typed, for example, a prewritten segment such as a paragraph or a sentence can be inserted from another file.

An industrial roofing contractor, for example, has a standard paragraph which is inserted into each bid. When the typist gets to the point in the bid document where the standard paragraph should be typed, a command will be issued to the system to transfer that paragraph from one file into the current document. This not only saves time, but if the paragraph is carefully worded to avoid possible misunderstanding and litigation, the transfer from one file to the current bid contract prevents typographical errors and omissions.

Another feature of word processing systems is the search/replace routine. The concept allows the computer to search for a letter, word, or phrase and replace them with another insertion. Once issued, the command is either performed automatically throughout the document with no user intervention or performed on each item found at the discretion of the user.

The controller sends out memoranda to all divisional managers reminding them of the upcoming budget process. Rather than sending one letter and photocopying it, a personal note will be sent each by name. There are 30 divisions and the same memo will be going to each one. The typist can issue a search/replace command and have a personal memo sent to each one by having one name replaced with another. Of course much of our current mail looks personalized based on this feature.

These are only a few features of a word processing software package. Now let's look at how the financial manager could benefit through the personal use of a word processor.

THE MANAGER'S USE OF WORD PROCESSING

Perhaps no software that is so commonly used has had more resistance toward its use by managers than word processing. Perhaps it is due to the equation of word processing with secretarial work. Maybe it is because of many managers' inability to touch type, or it could be due to a lack of understanding of the power of word processing, and where to apply it. Whatever the reason, there may be uses for word processing in the manager's purview that can be both productive and time-saving for him to personally use word processing. Some examples may help illustrate its potential.

Letter and Memo Writing Made Faster

Frank dictates numerous letters to business associates and colleagues. Frank likes the wording of these letters to be precise, so he reviews each of them before sending them out. If he has additions, modifications, or corrections to one, he makes corrections on the paper copy, and gives it back to his secretary for revision. Often he will read the letter a third time for composition, since the changes he has made are now easier to read in context. Sometimes Frank will ask for a revision to be done a second time (the third time a letter is typed).

Frank could find the word processing abilities of a microcomputer very helpful and time-efficient if he learned to use it in an appropriate manner. After dictation, his secretary could type the letter using a microbased word processing package and give it to him in the form of a diskette. Frank could edit the letter by inserting the appropriate wording and seeing it completely in context. Only one paper copy would be prepared, which would cut secretarial support time, and Frank would have to handle the letter only once.

Controlling Document Access

Helen must provide a written evaluation of each manager twice a year. It is company policy to keep the evaluation confidential so that only the individual manager sees his or her personal evaluation. To ensure confidentiality, Helen has handwritten each one usually more than once to get the exact wording.

Some managers would sympathize with Helen because, perhaps like her, they do not type and handwriting is presumed to be a faster mode of communication. However, it is generally faster to use the hunt and peck method of typing or the two-fingered approach rather than write the document out by hand. This is true for several reasons. Often people's handwriting is not very legible. Also, handwritten documents often require rewrite to clean up mark-throughs, erasures, and other corrections not desirable on a final draft. Again, handwritten corrections and changes are difficult to read in the context of the document, as they may be between lines, in different colored ink, or just hard to read. Word processing, even using two fingers rather than all 10, is often faster and more satisfactory than handwriting documents when confidentiality is desired.

Improvement of Grammar and Description

Junior accountants in any public accounting firm are required to write memoranda to the workpapers describing observations, audit procedures, or other activities which they or their colleagues have performed in an engagement. All of these memoranda are reviewed by the senior accountant(s) for completeness and correction. One of the complaints regarding these memoranda was that they were not complete in the description of the work done. Moreover, grammar was particularly displeasing, rendering some of the memoranda meaningless or misleading.

One of the more pleasing aspects of using word processing is that the junior accountant, who often presents a rough draft as a final copy, can now produce a better presentation faster. This phenomenon occurs because it is easier to modify paragraphs, sentences, and words with a few keystrokes than to rewrite an entire passage. Moreover, public accountants often have a time constraint, and rewriting becomes impossible if there is a budget to meet. Using a word processing software package gives the user an ability to quickly review a rough draft, make changes, and produce a final copy in a very short time. The senior accountant could review the document before it is in hard copy and make or suggest changes before it goes into the work papers.

In addition, the word processing department can receive a disk for financial statements and prepare the final firm release copy.

THE MANAGER'S SEARCH FOR A WORD PROCESSOR

Word processing software will often be promoted on the basis of its sophistication, power, and ease of use. To the professional typist these features have significance, even though they may have different meanings to different people. To the manager, however, the third feature, ease of use, should be of paramount importance when considering the purchase and use of a word processor. It is entirely possible that the need for a word processing package is unnecessary.

It is possible to use an electronic spreadsheet as a simple word processing package for short memos or brief draft documents. All one need do is begin in a cell that has no input currently in it or input in the adjacent cells to the right. Since a typical monitor has 80 columns, each line should not exceed that number and when 80 is approached, the text should be entered into the next line of the spreadsheet. What you now should see is one line of text across the screen. If you drop down to the next cell below the text and again type a line across it, you will have a memo that can be printed by making the print routine print only the several cells in that column. Of course, this approach is limited to items no longer than a few lines. However, if a manager is currently working on a spreadsheet application and recalls the need to send a brief interoffice memo to someone, all that is necessary is to drop down to an empty space on the spreadsheet, type the memo, and print the several cells.

Another approach is to use a memory resident software program (in Chapter 3) to pop up a window to type a note.

To ease the use of a spreadsheet as a word processor, one may set up a command file (referred to by different spreadsheet programs as a macro command or an execute file) which can be invoked so that the active cell moves to a remote part of the spreadsheet for the memo, another simple program can be written to type it automatically, and a third can erase the memo cells after its use.

The Lotus memo macro might look like

Name	Macro	Function
/G	'(GOTO) AA1	This sends the active cell to AA1(any other cell could be substituted)
/P	'/PPR(?)NGQ	This tells 1-2-3 to print on a printer a range provided by the user. (?) Replace this for actual range.
/E	'/RE(?)N	This tells 1-2-3 to erase a range provided by the user.

The manager's word processing package should be simple in its design, with features that the manager should be interested in. Having the ability to merge a document file with an address file (often referred to as mail-merge) is probably not a feature the manager should be interested in. Having the ability to insert special characters into text such as Greek mathematics symbols may not be useful, either. A word processor that makes input simple and output straightforward is often the best. The major exception to this rule is when the manager and secretary share documents for editing before a final draft. In this situation, it is better to choose a word processing package that meets the secretary's needs, since the secretary will be the primary user of the system. At least the secretary is there to answer any questions regarding the software's use.

One comment cannot be left unsaid. There will never be a word processing package that will completely substitute for the handwritten note. A handwritten note is often faster, may carry more meaning, and is always more personal.

Some word processing software can be very simple and others much more sophisticated. Also, some desktop publishing software will also be used for word processing. The choice should be based on what you want to do, where you want to do it, and who must do it.

An important rule, in using word processing, is to try to use the same software for the whole organization. Each one has different commands and when different kinds of software are used it becomes confusing when documents are transferred between people and when one secretary needs to help another. In addition, if documents are transferred between offices electronically (through modem) or by sending disks, using the same software makes use easier and faster. The commands established in the software is for special printing features can be used automatically if the same software is used. Too many times organizations allow all users to buy whatever they want, only to find out it causes mass confusion later. Personal computer freedom and organizational requirements have to be weighed against each other in this microcomputer area.

Some of the software available for microcomputer word processing systems are:

Displaywrite
Multi-Mate
PC Write
PFS Write
Peachtext
Samna Word
Wordperfect
Wordstar

In using any word processor or spreadsheet, it is very important to save your work by saving files. The data typed in is not automatically saved. You must remember specifically to provide the computer command to do this. Figure 6–1 indicates some tips for saving your work.

1. Save work, whether a report on word processing or spreadsheet, at least every hour. If the power fails, all work is lost unless it was previously saved.
   This is a very real and recurring problem

   TAG FOR COMPUTER

   HAVE YOU SAVED YOUR

   WORK

   IN THE LAST HOUR???

2. Save the same file on the same diskette periodically.
   Some software does this automatically for you.
   Many times the software asks:

   DO YOU WANT TO DO THIS?

   OR ASKS

   (Y/N)

FIGURE 6–1 Tips on saving work in office productivity software

7

TALKING TO THE WORLD: TELECOMMUNICATIONS AND EXTERNAL DATA BASES

Telecommunications move data from one physical location to another; in business the data that is there is frequently in a data base operated by one of the information utilities, but it could just as easily be an accounting or spreadsheet file on another microcomputer. A data base is a large, organized collection of data which may be searched for information on a particular subject. The searching is usually done with a data base management system, often incorrectly referred to as a data base. The data bases under discussion here are those external to your personal computer.

In the wide world of computers, telecommunication is generally abbreviated to telecom, but it means different things to different groups of people. Your company's mainframe data processing staff knows telecom primarily as high-speed direct line connections between large computers. For large corporations that operate many large- and medium-sized computers in many locations, telecom connects these computers into a theoretically seamless data exchange environment, albeit a rather expensive one. At this level, telecom is a complex and demanding specialty field in data processing.

In another context, telecom is frequently confused with the connection of computers into networks. Although you might be able to connect your computer to a network of computers using a telecom setup, without full-speed networking hardware and software your computer would be, at best, a junior member of the network.

For microcomputer users telecommunications means moving information via ordinary telephone lines; the implication is that a microcomputer is on at least one end of the line. Telecom in the microcomputer world is a fast and relatively inexpensive means of moving data long distances.

Although there are other tasks that fit the general microcomputer definition of telecom, the two tasks most likely to prove useful are:

Information retrieval (from a larger computer to a micro)

File transfers (between two microcomputers)

There is a separate chapter (Chapter 5) on data bases in this book.

INFORMATION RETRIEVAL—MICRO-MINI OR MICRO-MAINFRAME

Telecom is used in linking micros to mini or mainframe computers. The modem hook up can be used for retrieving information by saving the screen image that is shown by the mini or mainframe, then saved in a micro file. Or the file, if it is the correct size, can be sent to the micro. This access holds great potential for many new uses.

Many new packages have recently been developed and much additional development is needed to allow a nontechnical person to perform this function. Many times the hookup is made by the company's technical computer people, or computer consultant, and front-end menus and screens are prepared to facilitate other users to perform the same functions. Planning and development is important to use these connections in the appropriate way for the specific application and organization

FILE TRANSFERS BETWEEN TWO MICROS

Telecom can be used to transfer files between micros by the modem hookup. In this way many noncompatible computers can send files and similar software used in many locations can be coordinated.

One example is where a CPA firm is using the same audit software to audit a large company in a number of locations. In order to consolidate the final audited statements, telecom between the micros, used by the auditors at the various locations, can be connected to make this occur. When the local audit statements are completed, the auditor can telecommunicate them to the headquarters' auditors so they can save these files, then consolidate them through the use of the same audit software or through the use of another package such as a spreadsheet.

Networking, which is the transfer of information within a local environment (and not for long distances), can use modems; however, it is not part of this specific telecommunications discussion. Networking is important in the proper utilization of multiple microcomputers in the same organization and the sharing of common data on different computers. It is a separate technology in itself.

HARDWARE AND SOFTWARE FOR TELECOMMUNICATIONS

Additional computer hardware and software will be required to perform telecommunications. Both the hardware and the software are normal stock items with most computer dealers, and you will have the usual bewildering number of styles, prices, and features from which to choose.

Hardware required: Almost any standard business or personal microcomputer can be used for telecom. Generally, if it will produce the documents, it can telecommunicate them. Unless it has one built in, the computer will need a device called a modem. Modem is a contraction of MOdulator-DEModulator; the modem converts the computer's internal data representation into tones that can travel over the normal telephone system.

For use over common telephone lines, modems normally come in four speed ranges:

Up to 300 baud

1200 baud

2400 baud

9600 baud and up

Even higher speeds are under development by several manufacturers.

Baud is the speed rating and approximates the number of bits the modem can transmit or receive in one second. Since it usually takes 10 or 11 bits to send one character of information, a 1200 baud modem can be thought of as having the capability to move 120 characters per second.

Faster modems can also be used at slower speeds; you can use a 2400 baud modem at 300 or 1200 baud, if the computer you are communicating with supports only the slower speeds.

Although faster modems are more expensive, they send more data per time unit and they can also run at the slower speeds, making them more versatile. Buy a high speed modem; savings in long distance telephone charges can quickly repay the additional expense of a 2400 baud modem.

Although 300 baud was the standard speed for many years, 1200 baud is now almost universally supported, and 2400 baud service, although relatively new, is gaining wide support. There is a choice of line protocols. The Bell protocols are by far the most common; don't buy any modem that doesn't support them.

The new 9600 baud modems are most useful as a medium of file transfer from one micro to another because few of the information utilities are yet equipped with them. At this speed and above there is a diversity of modem line protocols (not to be confused with software data transfer protocols), so you need to seek out the latest in specific knowledge if you wish to enter the over-2400-baud arena.

If you will be communicating with computers in areas outside the United States and Canada, you should be aware that modem standards vary in different countries and are constantly changing. Three hundred baud is almost universal, but is very costly to use on long distance calls because of its slow speed. Higher speeds have different protocols in different parts of the world, and an expert's advice is necessary in this area.

Although many modem manufacturers provide software with their modems, most independently produced telecommunications software for microcomputers has been designed for modems that work like those manufactured by Hayes Microcomputer Products of Norcross, Georgia. These modems are made by many manufacturers, but are usually advertised as being Hayes compatible. This compatibility is important because the telecom software must send commands to the modem to control communications speed, telephone dialing, and the like. Unless you have software that you know will support other Hayes modem command protocols, restrict your choices to Hayes compatible units.

To further complicate your decision-making process, many modems are offered in variations of packaging; you may select an external modem (a separate box) or an internal modem that fits inside the computer. The external modem will require a serial port on the computer, some desk space (though most will fit under a standard desk telephone) and a place to plug into the wall. The internal modem will require an expansion slot on the motherboard and sufficient extra capacity from your computer's own power supply. Adding a serial port to the computer if there is not already one installed might use an expansion slot anyway, although it is possible for some computers to install a multifunction card with a serial port or two, a clock, a calendar, and additional computer memory. There is no performance difference between external and internal modems: 1200 baud is 1200 baud.

MODEM CHECKLIST

Speed	1200 baud or faster
Line protocol	Bell protocol appropriate to the speed of the modem.
Commands	Hayes compatible
Other features	Your choice
Mounting	Internal or external; see checklist below

MODEM MOUNTING PROS AND CONS

Internal and external modems are substantially identical in function, but there are some convenience and operational differences.

	Internal	External
Location	Inside computer, but only if there is space for it	Separate box
Connection	Internal to computer	Via serial port, which your computer may already have
Other hardware required	Usually none	Serial port, cable
Connecting cable (modem to computer)	None required	Required, but usually supplied. Some computers may require a special cable.

Installation	Computer must be opened, but otherwise straightforward	Just plug it in, unless you must add a serial port.
Power supply	From computer—check capacity	Separate power supply provided, usually requires a wall outlet
Convenience	More so than external, since it's always there	Can be used with other computers
Price	Generally lower than external	
Other advantages		Much better for portables: visible status lights
Failure rate	The same in either case, but internal modems are more difficult to remove for service. They are also harder to steal.	
Software required	The software itself, to be useful for the two major applications under discussion here, must be capable of file transfers with error checking and terminal emulation. Crosstalk and Crosstalk-XVI, developed by Microstuf, Inc., Roswell, GA, are widely considered the leading independently produced products of this type.	
Terminal emulation	Terminal emulation is the ability of the software to mimic the actions of a particular manufacturer's computer terminal. Terminal emulation is important when communicating with mainframe computers, information utilities, and data bases. The most popular terminal for these applications is the DEC VT-100 (and variations like VT-52 and VT-101) manufactured by the Digital Equipment Corporation. Many telecom software packages emulate other terminals, as well. Since business uses of telecom software almost invariably include access to large host computers, do not purchase any telecom software that does not	

emulate the types of terminals your mainframe can support in an asynchronous mode.

File transfers If, in your microcomputer in Seattle, you have a proposal that absolutely, positively has to be in Miami in 10 minutes, it is time to call on the file transfer abilities of telecommunications software. Using your computer, a modem, appropriate software, and the telephone, you can transfer that proposal to a similarly equipped system in Miami much faster than any courier. At 240 characters per second (2400 baud), it will take about 12 seconds per page. A good telecommunications program can send any type of file from one microcomputer to another, as long as both computers' telecom programs respect the same file transfer protocol or way of sending and receiving files. Whether the file will be meaningful to the computer receiving it is another matter and is not a function of telecommunications.

Files Everything stored in the modern microcomputer is stored in a system of files. Although conventions for assigning names to files vary among different types of computers, almost all computers have some system for naming various types of files. For example, each letter produced by the average word processing program can be stored in a file with a name meaningful to the computer operator. In fact, the word processing program itself is just another type of file.

File types There are two general types of files on a microcomputer: text files and binary files.

Text files Text files are made up entirely of printable

character (A-Z, a-z, 0–9, punctuation marks, and national symbols) and some special characters called control characters.

Binary files

Binary files include the text and control characters plus many more. These additional characters have no standard representation except for their binary values. Let us avoid the usual introductory course in binary math (something for which you are unlikely to find daily use) and merely state that a single byte may represent any one of 256 different alphabetic, numeric, or special characters. The first 128 characters of the 256 have standard meanings as text characters; the remaining 128 have meanings determined by the individual computer manufacturers. The last 128 characters are considered nontext. The presence of any nontext character in a file makes it a binary file. Many word processors save their files as binary files, as do most electronic spreadsheets.

Therefore, in order to transfer a proposal (made up of word processing and spreadsheet files), your software must have the capacity to send the file as blocks of binary data, not merely as individual characters. In addition, the software should perform some kind of error checking to assure that the data received in Miami is the same as the data transmitted from Seattle. This protocol varies among types of programs, but the best system involves the two software programs (one at each end of the line) in a considerable conversation. The form of the conversation varies, but usually follows the age-old guidelines for public speaking: Tell them what you're gonna tell them, tell them, then tell them what you told them. Between the two computers and their software, a conversation ensues that might go something like this:

Sending computer	Receiving computer
Ready?	Ready
Sending block 1 of 32	1 of 32. O.K.
Block will be 128 bytes long	128 bytes. O.K.
(sends 128 byte block)	O.K.
Computed checksum was 19784	19784. O.K.
Ready?	Ready

INFORMATION DATA BASES

Data bases are, as one might suspect, large amounts (bases) of information (data) more or less conveniently arranged and stored. The data in the data base is extracted or manipulated with a data base management system (DBMS). It is unfortunate that the term data base has been widely misused and has, in many peoples' minds, come to mean both the DBMS and the data it manipulates.

The topic here is data, stored in a computer, data you need and that is available over the telephone lines if you and the data base service operator can agree on the technical and financial requirements for access.

There are currently over 1000 data bases available via ordinary dial-up telephone lines. These data bases are maintained by various companies and governmental entities that can be found in most of the industrialized world. There is generally a charge levied for access to the data, but the methods used for determining the charges are as varied as the contents of the data bases themselves. One guide to the variety of data bases available is:

The Directory of Online Data Bases
Cuadra Associates, Inc.
Suite 305
2001 Wilshire Boulevard
Santa Monica, CA 90403

Many of the most popular data bases can be accessed through one of the information utility services. These organizations provide gateways to data bases maintained by other companies, and typically provide a unified method of searching the data bases for the data you want. Some of the more popular information utilities are:

Dow Jones/News Retrieval, operated by Dow Jones

CompuServe, operated by H & R Block

The Source, operated by Reader's Digest

Delphi, operated by Delphi

Dialog, operated by Lockheed

NewsNet, operated by NewsNet

NAARS, Nexis and Lexis, operated by Mead Data Central

Westlaw, operated by West Publishing Company

VU/TEXT, operated by Knight-Ridder newspaper

In addition the American Institute of CPA's provides a data base on accounting standards.

Each of these has its strengths and weaknesses. Dialog, for example, has probably the largest selection of data bases, but is somewhat complex. Lockheed offers a training course to teach professional information workers (i.e., corporate librarians and marketing researchers) how to use the service. At the other end of the ease-of-use scale is VU/TEXT, a full text data base containing newspaper stories from the Knight-Ridder papers, as well as Associated Press wire service stories.

These data base services act as organizers for the data they have available; most of the data is maintained by other, more specialized organizations. Some of the data bases themselves are accessible through more than one service.

Almost any microcomputer telecommunications software package will work with these and other data bases. Some of the data bases require that you have a certain type of terminal, like a DEC VT-100, but the better telecom software will emulate the response of various terminals, allowing you to use the same microcomputer to access several data bases regardless of the required terminals.

For some of the services there are special communications and processing packages available that help the infrequent user access the data base and use its facilities better. The most widely known of these is In-Search, a microcomputer package that simplifies interaction with the Dialog data bases.

When you sign up for the service, you will be given information on how to call in to the service's computer, how to use the service, and, usually, two sign-on codes: an account number and a password. The combination of an account number (like a street address) and a password (like a door key) prevents unauthorized persons from using your account. Since most, but not all, of the services assess an hourly charge for the time you spend on their computer, it is in your best interest to keep the password secret. Some rules for data base access:

Signing up — Your computer dealer or consultant knows whom to call if the necessary materials are not included with your telecommunications software. All the data base services make signing up relatively painless and, since they charge by the hour, they administer no computer competency tests: Your learning curve is at your expense.

Charges — Find out exactly how the service charges for your use of the system. Some charge by the minute, some the type of activity you perform, like a search. Differing styles of use can sharply reduce the cost of using a data base.

Sign-up charge — Generally, there is an initial fee to set up an account, then a schedule of fees for use. Most telecom software comes with sign-up kits and discount coupons for some of the more consumer oriented service. Some services allow you to sign up by calling their computer with your computer and authorizing your credit card company to pay your charges. You can be on-line in a few minutes.

Use charges — Most services charge by the connect hour: the elapsed time between when you sign on and sign off the service. Prices are generally lower at nights and on the weekends. Other fees are sometimes based on:

- The number of search requests
- The number of text lines sent to your terminal
- Pages printed on the service's computer

The amount of CPU (central processing unit) time you use. CPU time sounds very expensive (it can cost several dollars a second), but a large computer can do a lot of work in a second.

If you believe that you will be using the service extensively, call them human-to-human and find out the best way to use their system to get the information you seek. All the services have representatives who are willing and able to help you, and most have toll-free numbers.

Telephone access

Most of the services are available through one of the nationwide communications networks, making telephone access a local call in most cities. There are several of these networks, and some of the services are available on more than one network. Some of the networks are

GTE Telenet
Tymnet (McDonnell Douglas)
General Electric Information Services

The networks themselves have sign-on requirements, and you will need to know the network address of the service you want. Some of the services also assess a surcharge for using a third-party network; if there is an extra charge it will be listed in the schedule of fees published by the data base service.

Some of the data base services also have their own local numbers in major metropolitan areas.

If you access a service through a network like Telenet or Tymnet, you will be dealing with at least two layers (maybe 3) of communications, but once you sign on, it will be apparent to you.

If you are taking your computer with you when you travel, find out before you leave home the local number you will need to use to call your data base when you get to your destination.

Account numbers

Your account number is like your name and address on the data base service. If the service has an electronic mail facility, other users can send mail to you without having to know your password, but simply by sending it to your account number. Many services allow you to list yourself in a data base of users showing your interests and fields of expertise. If you list yourself in one of these directories, you put yourself in contact with other persons of similar interest.

Passwords

Change your password often and do not use your or your spouse's names or anything obvious or trivial. One major data base service used to give new customers a password consisting of the customer's city name. After several people found thousands of dollars of unauthorized use by people who had deduced the passwords, the data base began to issue more obscure passwords. Someone might find that account TRD 796 435 was in Albuquerque and, knowing the password assignment scheme, use the account. A password like UGANDA$FERRARI might be a little more difficult to guess.

DATA BASES AVAILABLE

There are so many data bases available that we can select only a few for mention here. Use the Cuadra Associates book mentioned above, or call a few of the data base services to find a more thorough discussion of the data bases available. Most of the data base services have a number of individual data bases on each of the topics below.

Subject	Data Base Services
Tax Information	NAARS
	NewsNet
	Dow Jones/News Retrieval
	Lexis
	Westlaw
Financial News	Dow Jones/News Retrieval
	VU/TEXT
	NewsNet

Financial News (cont.)	The Source
Annual Reports	Dialog
	NAARS
General News	Dow Jones/News Retrieval
	VU/TEXT
	NewsNet
	The Source
Corporate Acquisitions	NewsNet
	Dow Jones/News Retrieval
Information on Data Bases	Dialog
Stocks, Bonds, Commodities	Dialog
	NewsNet
	VU/TEXT's VU/QUOTE
	Dow Jones/News Retrieval
	CompuServe
	The Source

8

COUNTING ON SOFTWARE

COMPUTERIZED ACCOUNTING

Computerizing the old process of bookkeeping appears feasible for all, whether accounting for the small business, the doctor, the lawyer, or the Indian chief. There was basically no change in the debit and credit black book process until now. The computer age has drastically changed this. Large organizations have benefited from mainframe computers and minicomputers. However, the vast majority of small organizations received only minimal benefit by sharing larger computers through service bureaus and CPA write-up services. Microcomputers hold the incredible promise for the small business to automate its financial records.

For the first time, available at the user's fingertips, are faster and more accurate records, essential financial analysis, and necessary controls. Consider how long it takes someone to produce an accounts receivable aging from a large set of customer receivable cards. Practically any accounts receivable micro software package can print an aging minutes after it is requested. It's almost like enacting the Small Business Freedom of Information Act. However, we could spell that free doom. With freedom comes responsibility for one's own actions. In accounting this could spell disaster. The exhuberance that certainly should exist for the great potential of microcomputers must be counterbalanced by controls and proper accounting. The software will not make anyone know accounting, nor correct poor accounting procedures outside the computer. It can make a tool with tremendous potential power accessible. If applied properly, it can be that answer many are looking for.

Obviously, accounting software packages are purchased to be used. This is in contrast with office productivity software, much of which is never used. Those that are used are used many times in a limited fashion with many of the features never explored. These office productivity packages came with the hardware or just happened to be purchased due to its low cost.

Users of accounting software packages place much greater demands on all the features of accounting software. Software developers dealing with office productivity tools may not touch accounting packages. Accounting packages require accounting knowledge besides the knowledge of the package itself. Support becomes a two-dimensional problem—support of the packages as well as support of the accounting knowledge the software is based on. This is not to say it is easier to develop one product over the other or to maintain that product.

WHY COMPUTERIZE?

"My records were kept in this book for years. Why bother changing?" One change causes another. In our society we see the tremendous push for exercise and exercise paraphenalia stores, not just the exclusive spa. This was caused over the last 100 years by the change in our society and cardiac research more of a cause. We all sit too much. We go from the car in the garage at home to the garage at the office; then back home to watch TV.

Changes in our business world now make the computer a necessity in many cases.

There is much more reliance on communications.

Customers are farther away, not a buggy ride away, or even one day's car ride away.

Competition is increasing.

More information is available about competition and other important factors.

Society has become much more complex regarding analyzing more information for good business decisions.

There is more competitive pressure for fast delivery of services. Provision

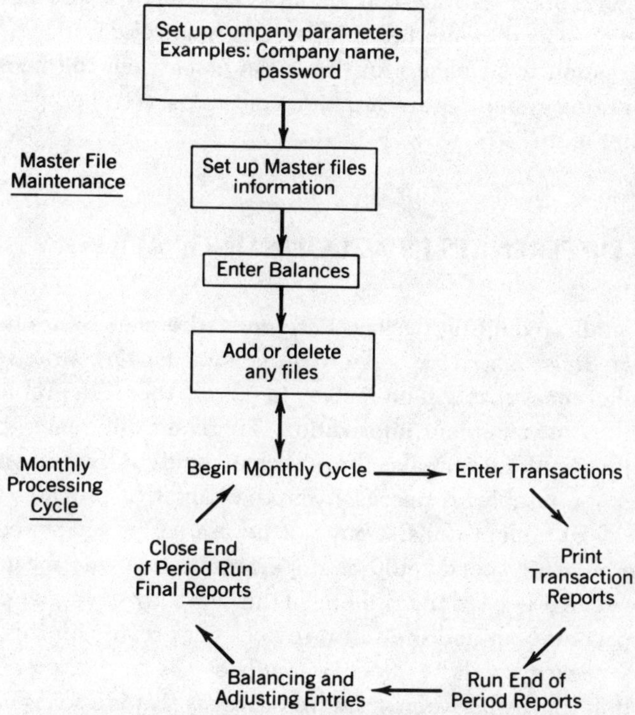

FIGURE 8–1 Chart for Computerized Accounting Systems

of such services requires instant knowledge of inventories, a sales order entry program, and faster processing of orders. First, we have one-day, then three-hour delivery. Can we now expect five minute deliveries, maybe through Star Trek-type transport machines?

Employees are more mobile and turnover is rising.

Mechandization and computerization exist in all other aspects of the business, in and around it.

As discussed in John Naisbitt's book, *Megatrends: Ten New Directions Transforming Our Lives,* we are in the Information Age. He talks about the impact computers will have. This information in the financial world can come from financial information being made available in computers; so the information can be processed faster, received faster, changed into different forms, and merged with other information. A simple example is where an inventory listing can be produced in minutes compared to hours or days.

The information to manage a business can come from the microcomputerized accounting system. Many are based on a basic accounting cycle structure shown in Figure 8–1.

DIFFERENCES IN ACCOUNTING PACKAGES

One may say all accounting packages are created equal. Basically, they all record transactions. A general ledger is a general ledger. This is not true. There are differences that will be the key to solving the main problem or will provide the key management information. There are differences that could cause a major problem or make the package significantly less valuable or possibly totally unusable. A microsoftware package that provides for a total dollar limit of 10 million dollars may not be usable for certain companies. Entry and processing speed could be important to some and meaningless to others and can be crucial to the running of the company. If an inventory must be kept by part number and the software does not provide for this, then not all inventory packages will be effective. Table 8–1 is an overview of some of the critical differences between software packages that are sold for the same purpose.

TYPES OF ACCOUNTING SOFTWARE PACKAGES

Basically, there are two general categories for accounting software. One is general purpose or generic and the other industry specific. In the early releases of microsoftware packages, one general ledger or one receivable package was offered. It became apparent that these packages could not be used by many businesses. Even if it could be used, many practices in the specific industry would limit its usefulness. One of the first vertical packages was CPA write-up. It was a modified general ledger package with a modified payroll software (called passive payroll, having no check writing ability) interfaced. It was designed to do many different companies' general ledgers. This is one of the first times in microcomputer use that speed became much more important than user friendliness. Such user friendly features as prompts for yes and no responses, required before being allowed to go on, slowed down a

TABLE 8–1 Example of Differences that Make a Difference in Accounting Software

General Areas Where A Difference Can Count	Examples
Industry specific	Accounts receivable package One for medical office allowing for third party patient rebilling. Not equal to a general commercial company with clients. Invoicing One invoicing for time (hourly rate) Not equal to one invoicing for goods in common commercial environment.
Ease of use	Ease of use is always talked about in microsoftware. However, it is different things to different people. Aspects of ease of use: Menu-driven Ability to avoid menu structure, go directly to entry screen, or report menu. Batch entry or interactive, that checks each entry as entered. Help facilities Clear and concise documentation Documentation on terminal Consistency of prompts, screens, function keys, etc. Quick to use by reference cards, tutors, help facility, etc.
Simplistic	A simplistic one-write system, very little changes A system with a range of options changed by user.
Powerful and flexible	A powerful data base system providing for different structures of files, multiple levels of changes by user, and a host of user defined reports.
Controls in the accounting software	Password control Allowing only authorized persons access to the system. Limit access to parts of system like master file maintenance compared to entry screen. Having entry editing Having processing controls, such as required backup when end of period is performed. Audit trails Transaction and file change reports Many other controls should be obtained. The importance of each depends on the specific company and application.

TABLE 8–1 (Continued)

General Areas Where A Difference Can Count	Examples
Dollar limitations	Transaction level limit Some packages will limit the largest dollar amount to be entered. Total dollar limit Some packages will limit total dollars to be effectively handled. Such as to a maximum dollars of $20 million. Or to total of $9,999,999.99 (9 digits).
Reports	Different reports available and ability to tailor reports to user needs by: Report generator Can provide for user to obtain very different types of reports without going into code of the program. Tie to electronic spreadsheet Can provide for different analytical reports and graphical presentations depending on the spreadsheet tied to. Tie to external report generator.
Speed	Processing of end of period Processing speeds for end of period depend on the software as well as the hardware. End of period processing may actually take hours even on a hard disk system. Entry of transactions Speed of entry could vary widely. Could depend on software being: Compiled or interpreted (if software code is in original readible form or is compressed). In batch mode or not Able to accept transactions one at a time or waits for a batch of data. Also may post one at a time Able to edit transactions one at a time or provide an exception report after group of transactions are quickly entered into the system.
General Ledger Account Limitations	If the accounting packages are to pass data to the general ledger, the same chart of accounts is needed. However, certain limitations exist. Can the software allow: Departmentalization Separate companies

	Cost center structure expense Allocation of more than one center Enough digits in chart of accounts— Total Number: 6, 8, 12 Sorting of accounts
Multiuser	Maybe essential in a company to have more than one person enter information in a file at the same time. Important for sales order entry.
Multitasking	Maybe essential that one person enters general ledger data, while at the same time another pays bills in the accounts payable package. Maybe essential that one person enters data, while another queries the files. Separation of duties is important to accounting.
Transfer of Data	Could be essential that all accounting software transfer data to others. Transfer to accounting data back and forth from office productivity packages. Important in updating budgets and graphic presentations of historical data.
Different Hardware	Other transfer of files may be needed Micro-Mini Micro-Mainframe Networking
Source Code Delivered	Some companies require the source code in case the vendor or dealer is not able or willing to support the software. In other cases, a simple modification in a report is useful (if license agreement allows). In still others, software is acquired as a base to a much larger tailored system. Software code could be: Delivered as part of the system Put in escrow by vendor Purchased separately Very difficult to obtain
Documentation	Good documentation and other aids outside the software are essential in applying it to the specific company's accounting system.
Help Facilities	Tutorials, help on the screen with use of PF key or reference card.

TABLE 8–1 Continued

General Areas Where a Difference Can Count	Examples
Updating of Periods	Require the accounting period to be closed before being able to enter data into a future period.
Entry	Require debits and credits to equal for each entry. May allow for unbalanced entry; however, requires trial balance to be in balance before financial statements can be printed or current period closed.

package, thereby becoming undesirable. The interactive features of many packages were used when batch processing was necessary. User friendly menus and submenus were not required; instead users were allowed to go directly to entry functions they wanted. Each user friendly feature should be reassessed based on the specific industry, user needs, and skill level.

Many problems can occur while using accounting software. To protect against these, operating procedures controlling access to the software, backups, and disk storage should be established.

A whole host of packages exist for the medical, retail, and distribution areas, just to name a few. A property management package can record what is owed just as in a receivable package; however, the concept is totally different because of the nature of the business. Many packages such as time and billing software, which can be used in a different business based on the need to bill on time instead of goods, blur the simplistic two-category concept. However, the use of the two categories allows quick understanding of the accounting software area and the attributes of a specific package.

The future holds the emergence of much more industry related software. This comes partly from the ability to write software from a common base of technology (program generators, which can generate program code, or a file handler) or from a predefined program, such as a DBMS program. Although the actual program coding chore may be getting easier, it is difficult to take shortcuts in industry knowledge. A medical package should deal with third party rebilling, and a banking general ledger should consider the level of daily transactions and methods of reconcilement.

In an industry specific package, knowledge must consist of:

- software
- accounting
- industry practices and standards.

GETTING STARTED

Obviously the first part of microsoftware use is the selection and installation process. (See Tables 8–2 and 8–3.) An enormous number of books, articles, and publications are available in this area. (See Chapter 10 for a detailed discussion.) It is just like having books on how to select a spouse. The selection process is important; however, it is the day-in and day-out activities that make life enjoyable or not. The same with software. No matter how good the software you have selected, you have to live with it day in and day out. Office productivity software can be a periodic tool, while accounting software is used within the monthly accounting process. Flashy software does not make it a better package in the day-to-day accounting process.

There are various issues that exist in the accounting microsoftware area:

1. Pricing is low so vendor cannot afford to spend much time with installation
2. The responsibility for installation rests on the user. Help should certainly be sought to ease this problem significantly.
3. Microcomputers are evolving faster than most other computer technology.
4. The low cost of much of this technology provides a false sense of security and ease of use.
5. The low cost has even created a throw-away philosophy. If it works, it works; if not, take it out. In certain limited cases this may work. However, if the effort and funds are expended, then a commitment for success should be made. The possibility for failure may create failure. If computerizing an important part of the accounting function is undertaken, then the benefits should be significant enough to provide for this commitment. In addition, the time investment taken to put in a system is one that could have been expended somewhere else.

Three major attributes the people who will deal with the software must have is:

Patience, patience, patience

Flexibility

Time

Normally this process is new. If someone is pressured into getting a new system, then failure is more likely than success. Each accounting software

TABLE 8–2 Steps in the Microcomputer Marriage and Ideas for Avoiding a Divorce

Courtship

Selection Process

1. Plan Preinstallation
2. Analyze
   - Needs that can reasonably be fulfilled by a microcomputer
   - Information required out of system
   - Current system
   - Changes to current system
   - Future
   - Budget constraints and other restrictions
3. Help
   - Get help if needed
   - Internal company consultant
   - Company's CPA or other consultant
   - Business computer dealer
4. Evaluate
   - Evaluate software first
   - (See Chapter 10 on purchasing computers)
   - Consider compatibility issues and many others
5. Alternatives
   - Determine alternatives
   - In this process should determine:
     - Leave system the way it is
     - Stay manual
     - Go to larger computer system
6. Price
   - Now can talk to computer salesperson about price
7. Other
   - Other steps needed to be performed
8. Decision
   - Make selection of system and decide on all surrounding considerations

Marriage Ceremony

Installation

1. Plan installation
2. Change
   - Change accounting system outside computer where needed or desired
3. Conversion of data
4. Perform installation
5. Train
   - Train many different people

TABLE 8–2 Continued

6. Run system and compare to old system
7. Other

Honeymoon

Postinstallation

1. Plan postinstallation review
2. Perform review and tests
3. Change other parts of system outside computer
4. Make revisions in software or hardware as required
   (Note: The above list is specific for accounting applications. Chapter 10 describes a more general approach.)
5. Other

package is different and accounting by the utilization of a computer, even a micro, can be a totally different process than maintaining manual records such as customer accounts receivable cards or posting to a black general ledger book. Sometimes the previous bookkeeper or accountant will retire or just leave. Using accounting software even on a microcomputer certainly is not automatic but it is still accounting. Being patient and dealing with the problems one by one without blaming the software, hardware, or operator provides a better chance for success.

Dealing with microcomputers requires flexibility. Normally you do not receive exactly what you want. It is not a custom package and the people writing the system do not know the specific company's procedures or personnel. There will be some bending needed to fit the software into place.

Be sure you need to perform all the tasks on the microcomputer. There are many processes in a particular company that should not be automated or automated through other means. (See Figure 8–2). Don't force it when it is not a good fit.

Time should be allocated to select and install the software. If not spent in the front end, much more can be spent in the back end.

BEFORE STARTING

Be sure not to continue the mistakes of the past! Do not computerize a bad manual system. Changes must be made before computerizing. This is a time to evaluate the accounting system; the opportunity should not be passed up.

TABLE 8–3 Tips on Running Dual Systems
Comparing Output in the New System to the Old

1. Admit to the need for this task before computerizing.
2. Plan for it.
3. Hire temporary help if necessary. Normally, there are no extra people around to run both systems at the same time. Current staff already have full-time jobs. In small companies, there is usually only one person who performs the tasks to be automated. A temporary employee supervised by the person responsible for the new system could provide that extra help during this period. The temporary can be a data processing input person or from an accounting temporary agency.
4. Set aside certain nights and weekends as part of the plan to be sure it is worked on compared to other work.
5. Verify input or all historical data. Most times historical accounting data has to be entered into the system first, like accounts receivable customer information, general ledger chart of account numbers or inventory activity, and balances on-hand. Obviously bad historical data will create havoc. Verify the historical data before entering. Most packages allow entry directly into the master files through master file maintenance.
   Consider: Entry of opening balance beginning of year then all current year historical data through normal transaction entry, close out each time period, and verify before continuing entry routine. Verify historical data entered before running dual. Historical data entry can be facilitated by the use of a temporary clerk or electronic transfer of data from the old media to the new.
6. Balance all end of periods involved. These include: End of day or week, End of month, End of year (could use prior year data).
7. Run dual systems by using prior periods. Enter prior period into computer as if it is a current period. This approach allows the process to be entered over a much shorter time, sometimes a month. However, wait for the one current period entered also.
8. Involve those responsible for the system day to day. They should be entering some or all of the data. Also a formal sign-off on the system indicating the information balances is useful.
9. Be prepared to take longer than expected.
10. Don't hold up process by one definable problem. If there is a definable problem not affecting any other area, consider putting the system in place.
11. Be honest with yourself. Evaluate system knowing it is the last time to stop the use of the new system and the end of the old.

FIGURE 8–2 Company A

Planning Chart for Alternatives in Computerizing Accounting Systems on Microcomputer

	General Ledger	Accounts Receivable	Accounts Payable	Payroll
Stand Alone				
Microcomputer				
Single User				
One Write				
Common double entry				
Stand alone				
Integrated	XXX	XXX		
Sophisticated				
Data Base Structure				
Multitasking				
Multiuser				
Ties to Other				
Computers				
Networking				
Microcomputer to Minicomputer				
Microcomputer to Mainframe				
Combinations				
Microcomputer to service bureau				
Microcomputer to CPA write-up service				
Others				
Manual			XXX	
Service bureau				XXX

Doctor A Planning Chart for Alternatives in
Computerizing Accounting Systems on Microcomputer

	General Ledger	Medical Office	Claims Procedures	Payroll
Stand Alone				
Microcomputer				
Single user				
One write				
Common double entry stand alone		X		
Integrated				
Sophisticated Data Base Structure				
Multi-tasking			X	
Multi-user				
Ties to Other				
Computers				
Networking				
Microcomputer to Minicomputer				
Microcomputer to Mainframe				
Combinations				
Microcomputer to service bureau				X
Third party rebilling to Medicare				
Microcomputer to CPA write-up service	X			

Corporation C & Outside Sales Offices

Planning Chart for Alternatives in Computerizing Accounting Systems on Microcomputer:

	Dates for Implementation And Changes in Current Microcomputer System			
	Sales Order Entry	Inventory	Accounts Payable	General Ledger
Microcomputer				
Single user				
One Write				
Common double entry				
Stand alone				
Integrated				
Sophisticated				
Data base Structure				
Multi-tasking	Currently in place		Currently in place	5/31
Multi-user	7/25			
Ties to Other *Computers*				
Networking				
Microcomputer to Minicomputer				
Microcomputer to Mainframe				
* Query information		6/30		
* Transfer Data at end of day	8/25		8/25	10/25
Combinations				
Microcomputer to service bureau				
Microcomputer to CPA write-up service				
Others				
Manual				

Table 8

—3 indicates some tips during this system verification stage.

Get as much out of the new investment as possible. You should consider new management information, new controls, and more details.

A computer system certainly can be added to later and should be part of the initial plan. Because of changes in technology, this can become an evolving process, not an effort forgotten about during the next century. Add hard disks, modems, and word processing, but do not try to do everything today.

Start simple! You may end up accomplishing nothing or, worse yet, destroying part of the accounting records.

The basics of the accounting system have to be mastered first, then proceed. Try to maintain simple structures and simple technology the first time, if going from a manual system. As an example create a simple chart of accounts that can be used. Make reports understandable.

The fear factor has stopped many a system from being purchased or installed successfully. An example of change in this is the computer salesperson who, seeing a reluctancy on the part of the decision-maker, decided to leave a microcomputer and software with a customer. The decision-maker, without anyone watching, used the computer and software at night. An understanding of what the salesperson was trying to explain became self-evident. This self demo made him comfortable with the micro. People do not like to look foolish and the computer is still intimidating. Once a person uses it and sees that there is nothing to fear except fear itself, the technology is welcomed.

Be sure time is spent on training. Training can be an ongoing process, based on turnover and additional people needing to use the system. Even though it is a microcomputer, training is still very important and the best training is hands on. Touching the keys, bringing up the menu, and printing reports are all part of the process of learning a system and surpassing the fear factor. Sample company data should be used. In this way the system can be used without any effect on the company's financial data.

We have all made accounting on microcomputers look too simple on the one hand, and significantly underapplied on the other. When the system is not up and running quickly, the boss may get upset and believe that the operator is incompetent. Then the operator tries to get the system working sooner then it should or find excuses why the machine is at fault. The reality is that accounting is still being performed and a machine called a microcomputer is used. It takes time and knowledge for it to work properly.

Don't let anyone practice software without a license.

DAY-TO-DAY LIVING

Controls are important in any accounting system. In fact, they are even more important in computerized systems.

A common syndrome is that someone reading financial statements believes:

A computer printout is accurate.

A typed report may be accurate.

A handwritten report is not accurate.

A computer statement can be just as bad as the handwritten or just as good. A great deal of it depends on the controls. A poorly designed accounting system that is automated will give no better results. People should not be allowed to make entries without sign off by an authorized individual or cash not entered and checks written without a bank statement reconciliation, just as it should be in a manual system. The computer cannot tell if someone wants to enter a $5,000 invoice instead of a $50 one. Therefore, proper manual controls outside of the computer are a critical part of the process in using software. The internal controls detailed in books like *Montgomery's Auditing* are as meaningful in computer systems now as in manual. People give too much credit to the computer, then are disappointed with the reality of what it can do. (Although it is doing more each day.)

The following are only examples of some controls for maintaining integrity and accuracy of the system. More complete discussions on these controls can be found in accounting texts.

Input Control Sheets

The input control sheet compares total dollar amounts at the source of creation to the end of day, week, or month records output.

EXAMPLE: SALES ORDER SYSTEM

1. Sales order is copied directly after completion by salesperson and sent to control clerk.
2. Copies are checked for completeness, totaled daily, and entered onto monthly control sheet.

3. Daily computer amounts compared to input tape.
4. Control sheet is totaled at end of month.
5. Reconciliation form is completed to compare these original document totals to the sales totals from the computer system. This is like reconciling your bank statement.
6. The items that could create a difference between the amount booked and the sales shipped are:

   Back orders from last month shipped this month.

   Back orders this month.

   Orders taken last month (or any previous month) and shipped this month.

   Orders taken but not shipped this month. (This is important to know. Normally, the slower the shipments, the slower the cash receipts, especially if on COD basis or receivable Net 30 from date of receipt.)

   Mistakes on original order such as math extensions or footings, pricing, or incorrect inventory numbers.

The above may have to be compared by units if computer generates dollar amounts or a total dollar amount calculated.

Batch Control Sheets

This is another method of reconciling input to output.

Batch control sheets compare total dollar amount of transactions entered to transaction computer printout.

EXAMPLE: ACCOUNTS PAYABLE ENTRY OF BILLS

1. Make tape of total amount for bills to be entered that day.
2. Post amount to batch control sheet.
3. Make sure the daily transaction printout is prepared. (Many software packages allow this as an option to print.)
4. Write total of transaction amount on sheet and compare to control tape total. Explain any variances.
5. This could be done by just keeping the original, nonedited tapes with no control sheet and initialing the transaction printout. This will have to

be done by batch number or verification that only one batch a day is processed.

Monthly Transaction Reconcilement

Monthly transaction reconcilement compares amounts personally approved to printouts of transactions.

EXAMPLE: RECONCILE CASH OUT

1. In authorizing weekly cash payments write total cash out you personally approved, on monthly reconcilement form. This could be done weekly depending on level of activity.
2. At end of day, week, or month compare this total to the accounts payable computer printout or other verifiable computer printout.
3. When other cash is disbursed from one preestablished authorization (such as automatic bank withdrawal for payroll or monthly interest), then modify steps or only use a computer printout that would logically compare to authorized amounts.

Previously Used Controls Verifying Amounts

EXAMPLES

1. Bank reconciliations and comparison to general ledger.
2. Physical inventories of goods and comparison to amount in general ledger or by category.
3. Inventory of fixed assets and comparison in detail. The above steps will not help find fraud; however, they are examples of simple procedures that can be used to control input and output.

CONTROLS IN SOFTWARE

Accounting software has many internal controls programmed into the system. There is no standard for the controls needed in the software. Some packages are very weak in this area and others are very strong. Normally, vendors are consistent in the controls within their software offerings, or certainly should be over time. Controls vary from stopping the user from crashing the system to requiring balancing debits and credits in an entry. Some can relate to all accounting software and others to specific types of accounting. No matter; controls in accounting software are a very important part of producing accurate records and providing for proper audit trials.

Certain controls are very useful in general to protect from loss of data and other errors the user can accidentally cause. These include requiring an automatic end-of-period back-up diskette to be created while performing this procedure.

Controls can vary as much as the user desires to have them. Just because a control is useful does not make all users want it. In fact, vendors have to deal with the desires of users for flexible utilization on the one hand and necessary controls on the other. A case in point is allowing a user to change records directly through master file maintenance, instead of entering a transaction requiring an audit trail. This was a battle raging at the beginning of 1980 in the early days of microcomputer utilization. An acceptable resolution of this was for the vendor to have a two-tiered password system so one password could be allocated to master file maintenance at installation, then changed or totally deleted. Therefore, the software provided for the controls; however, the user had the flexibility of deciding the level of controls. In many situations, accounting controls make it harder to use, and thus sell, the software. However, they are very important in the maintenance of any type of accounting system.

Three-year Car Obsolescence Theory

Obsolescence is a fact of life in the microcomputer field. All businesses accept the necessity of replacing the $10,000 company car every three years. However, these same companies expect to buy a microcomputer that will last forever. Use the micro, depreciate it over three years, and then throw it away, trade it in, keep on using it, or use it for another task. In the minicomputer world, certain computers are traded in; now in the micro area, selling certain used micros is becoming feasible. The new touch screen doesn't make your previous ability to do basic accounts payable any less feasible. In fact, after two or three years what we see is the older computers being placed in other areas of the company for word processing or electronic spreadsheet use. By this time, the company needs two or more micros anyway.

The obsolescence fear needs to be reduced to allow computerization of manual books to go forward quickly. Cars don't last forever, so why should microcomputers, especially when they will take the company further?

Single User or Multi-User

Based on the increased power of the microcomputer, more than one person can work with the same accounting system.

If only one person can access the files on one computer it is single user. However, many accounting applications are multi-user where more than one person can enter into accounts receivable or any other accounting package at the same time. See Chapter 14 concerning Multi-user considerations.

9

PRESENTATION MICROSOFTWARE AND OTHER SOFTWARE TOOLS

THE SOFTWARE TOOLBOX

There will always be new software on the market to make the microcomputer more functional and more valuable. Two kinds of office productivity software are significant, even though they are not part of the Big Three (i.e., word processing, spreadsheets, and database management). One works with each of the major software classes and is available at the touch of a keystroke or two. It is referred to as RAM resident or memory resident software. The other is made up of miscellaneous utilities that perform numerous, useful, and varied functions. Both have become important office productivity tools.

Memory Resident Software

RAM resident software is loaded into random access memory and can be called up out of memory for use with another software package. Often RAM resident software programs are entered into the computer's memory automatically when the unit is initially turned on or "booted." They can be, for example, keyboard enhancers or the very popular desktop utilities. Keyboard enhancers can vary from those that work with a particular software package such as spreadsheet software to those that work with the operating system to exercise several commands sequentially. These enhancers may allow several keystrokes (representing commands) to be programmed into just one keystroke. The series of spreadsheet commands—Print, Align, Go, Quit—can be expressed as a spreadsheet macro or execute command, or they can be programmed through the keyboard enhancer to be issued when pressing a single letter—P, for example.

Of greater interest to microcomputer users has been the desktop utilities that have been written under several names. These software packages are also memory resident and can be very useful in certain situations. The memory resident software resides behind the application being used and, upon a keystroke, the application screen becomes frozen while the resident program is activated through a window. Desktop utilities get their name from the attempt to remove the typical devices that are on the manager's desk including: the calculator, a personal telephone list, a desk calendar, an appointment calendar, a notepad (or scraps of paper used as a notepad), and a typewriter. A brief description of each of these desktop functions follows:

THE CALCULATOR FUNCTION: Is almost self-explanatory. Upon request, a hand-held calculator appears on the screen complete with memory, clear, and clear entry buttons along with the number pad. Two features are available on better calculator functions: (1) a tape that displays the entries along with the total so that one doesn't have to remember whether a number has been entered or not, and, (2) the ability to transfer the total to the currently used application. This latter feature allows the user to add, subtract, multiply, and divide a list of numbers and to take the total and transfer it to a spreadsheet or word processing package at the point of the cursor. This feature transfers the exact number obtained, which avoids transposition errors when copying the number into the application manually.

THE TIME/DATE FUNCTION: May have its major use when the hardware does not have an automatic clock/calendar board. However, its functions are useful if one wants to have an alarm signal at a particular time, such as a reminder for a scheduled appointment. Some will allow the automatic execution of a command or series of commands through an autoexecute file at the time of the alarm. Without a clock/calendar board, the function eases the setting of the time and date for file purposes and will usually display the current time in the upper right hand corner of the screen.

THE CALENDAR FUNCTION: Will often have two functions. One can view the current month, the past months, and future months for a particular day/date combination. Often the calendar is associated with a notepad so that, for example, appointments can be scheduled or specific projects due can be noted. Some calendar notepads will have times of day printed on the left hand column so the user can insert names or places of appointments at the specific time. Of course, these notes can be printed so that they can be inserted into one's pocket calendar.

THE OPERATING SYSTEM: Allows the user access to operating system commands such as Checkdisk, Checkdirectory, Directory, and Erase among others, while using an application program. Without this function, the user would have to exit the application program and access the operating system.

A NOTEPAD FUNCTION: Allows the user the opportunity to make a note at any time electronically. Remember the idea you had that was lost because you didn't have a scrap of paper to note it on? The notepad function provides a screen to make notes, save them, and print them out later while you continue to work on the application package.

THE PHONE DIALER FUNCTION: Allows the users to store their personal telephone book and, with the use of a modem, dial a telephone number automatically. Current telecommunications equipment often will have the capability to program frequently called numbers, but there is a limitation to many dialer functions. Due to the size of the directory one may have, some dialer functions will have a search capability which allows the user to seek a set of indicator letters or numbers for a match. This allows the user to automatically obtain a number without manually scrolling through a list. If the indicator letters follow a pattern, it will allow the user to enter new names and numbers in any order without alphabetizing them. For example, if JRO consistently means the first initials of a person's name and the last letter means office, the name John Rowell and his office number can be added to the end of the list and the automatic search can be activated.

THE PRINTER CONTROL FUNCTION: Will send commands to a dot matrix printer which will allow compressed, emphasized print, double width, and other print features. Again, the advantage is that one does not have to learn the application package being used to send a printer string from the operating system. The typewriter function: Allows the microcomputer and the printer to become an electronic typewriter. This function is useful for typing labels and addressing envelopes, among other applications.

Example of some of these memory resident software functions are shown in Chapter 3, Integrating and Using Spreadsheet Power.

Miscellaneous Utilities

The microcomputer and its software are merely tools to help people do their jobs more efficiently and effectively. Utility programs speed the process and are convenient for the user. Utility software must be used with other software, particularly the operating system, to be of benefit to the manager/user. Utility programs help solve the small, frustrating, time-consuming computer problems. Some of the currently available utility programs are:

Utilities that will recover files that have been erased in error.

These utilities can be used for files that have been erased using the Erase or Delete commands.

Utilities that set aside a part of RAM as a printer buffer so that documents may be directed to the buffer and spooled (sequentially fed into the printer) while the microcomputer is released for other uses. In other words, these utilities allow the simultaneous printing of documents while the user continues to use the microcomputer.

Utilities that set aside a part of RAM as an electronic disk for a second (b:), third (c:), or fourth (d:) drive. Rather than accessing the floppy disk, the user has a speed disk for faster processing. Of course, any files created on the electronic disk must be copied to a floppy or hard disk before turning off the unit.

Utilities that allow the deletion or copying of a selection or series of files rather than exercising the command numerous times for each file to be deleted or copied.

Utilities that allow the full screen browsing of a file using up, down, left, and right arrows to move the cursor.

Utilities that allow the user to scroll a file both forward and backward along with the ability to recall a screen for further reference. These utilities are especially useful if one is working on a segment of a worksheet but needs to refer to another part of the worksheet continually. With a keystroke, the referenced segment of the worksheet is in view without affecting the work being done.

The following utilities are especially valuable for hard disk users.

Utilities that search all directories and subdirectories for a particular file. This is particularly useful when several directories have been created with files in each one.

Utilities that allow the user to change file attributes so that files may be hidden, read only, or normal. Directories and subdirectories can be hidden also. When files, directories, or subdirectories are hidden they will not show up using the directory (DIR) or tree (TREE) commands. These utilities are very useful if the user has files or directories that are personal or confidential.

Utilities that allow the user to convert files to read only, preventing the accidental erasure or deletion of a file.

Utilities that allow the user to request a file directory to be displayed sorted by extension, size, date/time, or normally. This type of utility will also present a directory with comments beside each file for easy reference.

There are many other utilities that save time; manage files; convert files from, for example, C/PM to DOS; or speed printing commands.

These and other utilities are available from software vendors or they are often available in the public domain. For information on public domain software contact a local user group, or if one is not available for the IBM PC and compatible contact PC-SIG (Special Interest Group), 1030 East Duane Avenue, Suite D, Sunnyvale, CA 94086. For MacIntosh public domain software contact The Public Domain Exchange, 673 Hermitage Place #1A, San Jose, CA 95134.

A number of the utilities previously mentioned work with or supplement the utilities in the operating system. The MS-DOS operating system, for example, provides several utilities that may be useful as well. One should review the manual accompanying the operating system commands, as it may be of value.

SOFTWARE FOR BUSINESS PRESENTATIONS

Graphic pictures are often more explanatory than verbal presentations. Textual material along with graphic presentations get the message across more quickly and with less misunderstanding. In the past, graphic presentations have taken the form of bar charts, pie charts, line graphs, and other variations of these types. These charts were often difficult to draw by hand because of scaling problems and because the time necessary to develop professional charts was lengthy. These difficulties were largely reduced with the introduction of the Lotus 1-2-3 spreadsheet, which combined graphics presentations with the electronic spreadsheet. With the issuance of a few commands, one could see financial data immediately presented on the screen several graphical ways. With another series of commands, a printed copy of the graph could be available on a graphics printer. This feature in 1-2-3 was further enhanced with the release of Lotus HAL. Besides this type of software there are dedicated graphics software. Lotus itself produces one named Graphwriter.

Having a graphics software program, even the right program for the user, does not eliminate the need to carefully judge the appropriateness of the graphs one chooses to illustrate the data.

In the three charts (Figures 9–1, 9–2, and 9–3) financial data were taken from the illustration in the chapter on spreadsheets of the company with three different products. The purpose of the graph was to demonstrate the relative actual sales to the two years estimated sales. By looking at the three charts, one can see that the line chart and the pie chart show three distinct products, but none of them best illustrates the relative size of the products sales to one another. The line chart shows each of the three products as a box, a diamond, and a plus sign. However, no indication is given on the graph as to which of the products goes with each symbol. The pie chart is even more confusing, and while it shows the relative percentages of products A, B, and C to a total, it gives no indication whether these relationships are for 1986 actual, 1987 estimated, or 1988 estimated. In fact the pie chart sums all of 1986, 1987, and 1988 sales revenue together by product and takes each of these years to the total of all sales for the three years. The bar graph illustrates most clearly the information desired. Note that each of the graphs were drawn using the exact same limitations: sales by product by year. It should be clear that the user must judge the appropriateness of the graph given the information to be illustrated.

The success of Lotus' integrated software package and its limitations have

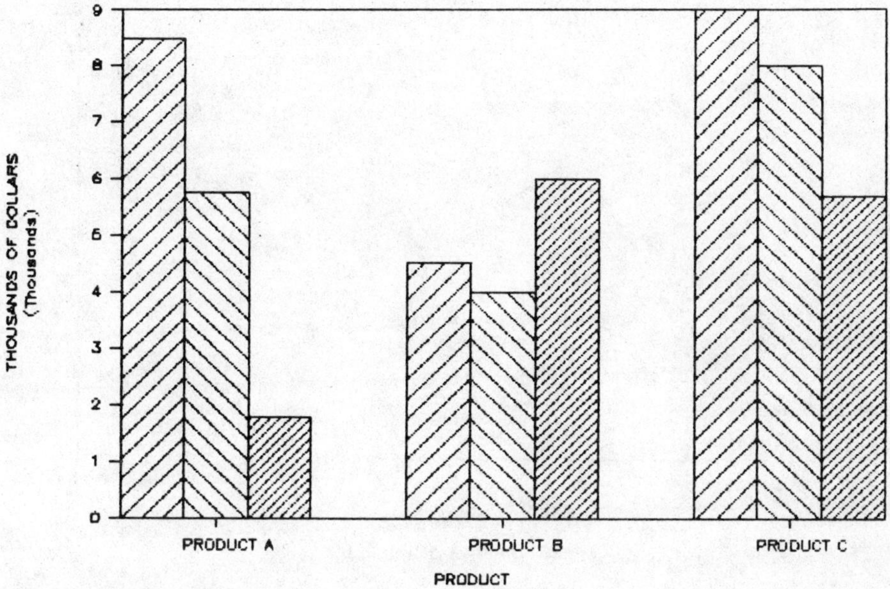

FIGURE 9–1 Example A

prompted software developers into a number of projects that have led to business graphics packages which display numerical data in a picture presentation and provide hard copy. These packages have several features that improve on the original Lotus concept. Graphics programs seem to fall into several categories that divide along the lines of features one program has compared to another.

Some of the graphics programs enhance graphs created by the electronic spreadsheet programs. For example, they can make presentations of financial data with horizontal bars rather than vertical ones. They can provide three-dimensional charts along with the more conventional single-dimension ones created by the spreadsheet software. Other graphics programs stand alone, and data must be entered before a graph or chart can be drawn. These can be useful if data are being generated from several programs, including spreadsheets and database managers.

Another kind of graphics program allows the use of more than line drawings. Prepared pictures, letters in a variety of fonts and font sizes, and the ability to draw pictographs on screen are a few of the features of these software programs (see Figure 9–4). Again, the idea is to get the message

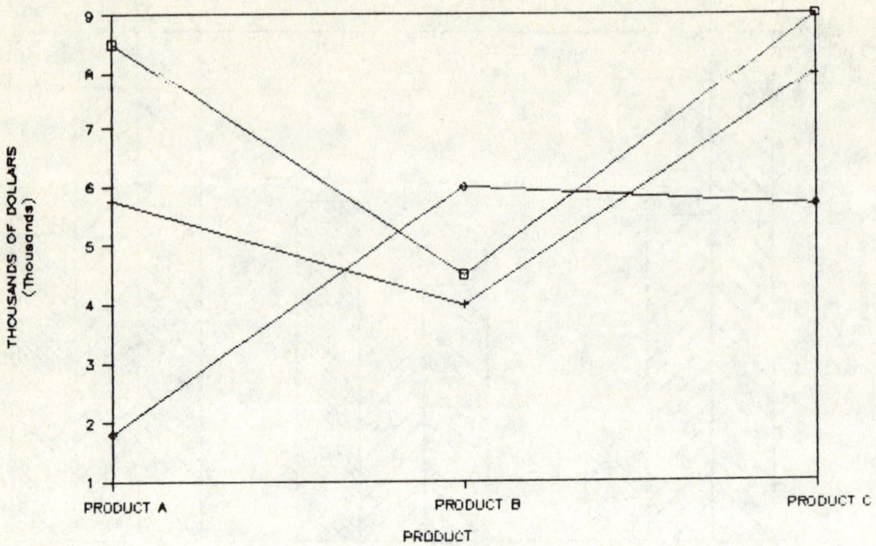

FIGURE 9–2 Example B

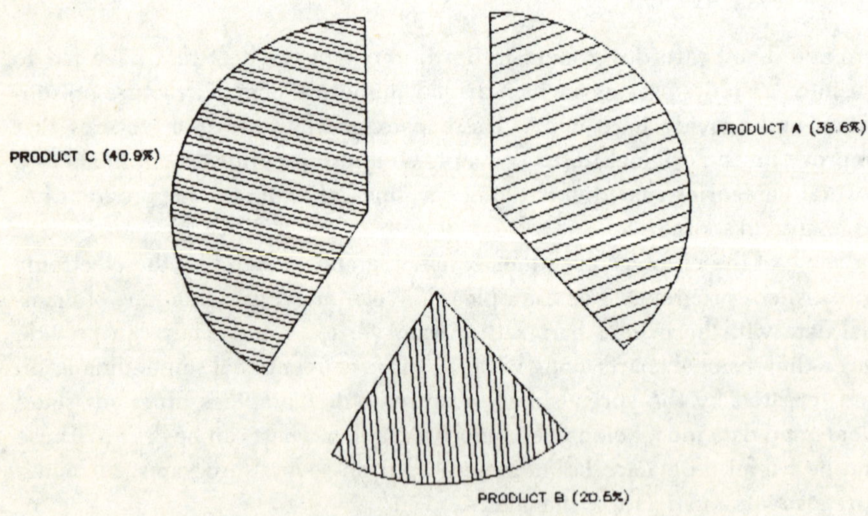

FIGURE 9–3 Example C

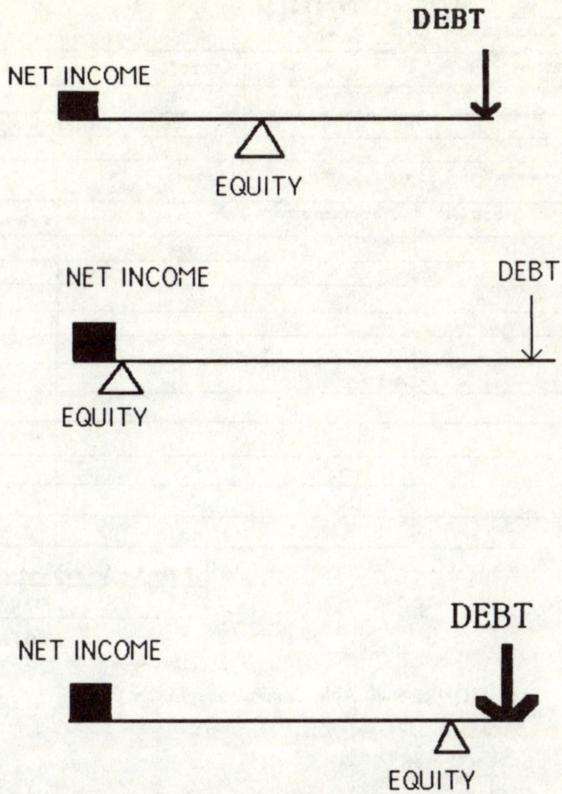

FIGURE 9–4 Net Income/Equity/Debt

across more effectively. These programs, when coupled with the appropriate hardware, can produce 35mm color slides and print transparencies: they can also produce printed quality documents with a laser printer. Some of these programs are able to provide simpler forms of animation to be presented on a computer along with an oral presentation.

There are a number of factors the manager must consider before investing in a graphics program.

Quality of the Graphics Output: Most dot matrix printers can print graphics output, but the quality is generally less than adequate. If quality output is needed, additional hardware may be necessary. Color plotters or

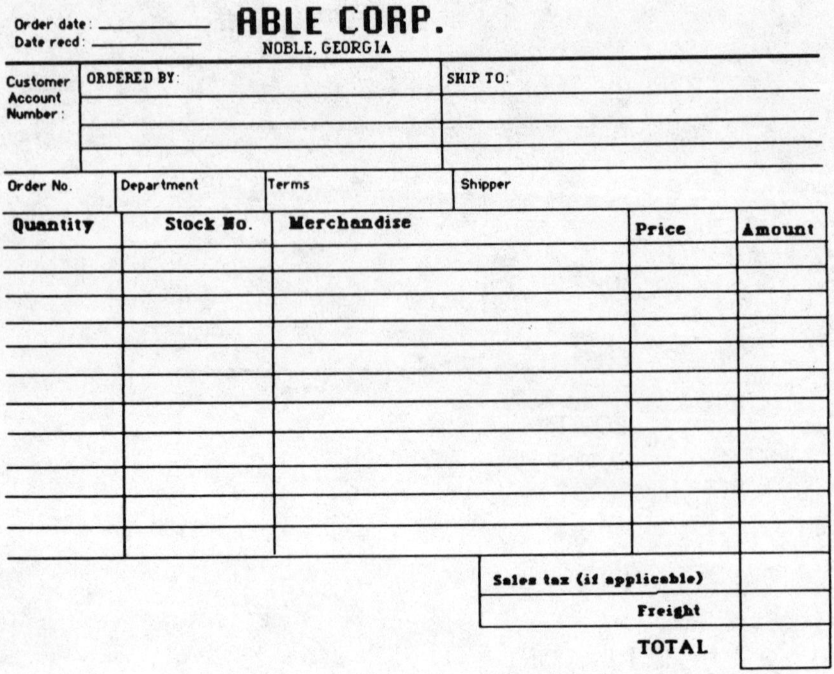

Order date:
Date recd:

ABLE CORP.
NOBLE, GEORGIA

Customer Account Number:	ORDERED BY:	SHIP TO:

Order No.	Department	Terms	Shipper

Quantity	Stock No.	Merchandise	Price	Amount
			Sales tax (if applicable)	
			Freight	
			TOTAL	

FIGURE 9–5 Able Corporation Order Form

printers, laser printers, and color monitors may be needed along with the software.

VERSATILITY OF THE GRAPHICS OUTPUT: Most integrated spreadsheet programs with a graphics feature will produce line, pie, or bar charts only. If there is a need for other types of presentation graphs, a software program with those options should be sought.

NONTRADITIONAL GRAPHICS OUTPUT: Most business graphics software includes traditional charting output (bar, line, pie). For firms that need nontraditional output such as flowcharts, pictographs, and printing, specialized software should be considered. When this type of software is required, the software package should support the use of a mouse or handheld device that allows freehand drawing or selection of optional icons (pictures representing a function) on screen. Figure 9–5 is an example of an invoice designed with the use of graphics software and a mouse. One can see that the design of forms can be facilitated by having the correct software.

DEDICATED GRAPHICS WORK STATION: A problem with using graphics programs is the expense of the hardware necessary to adequately support the software. Further, users often do not continuously need or use graphics packages as they might use electronic spreadsheets, for example. Therefore, the manager may consider setting up a single workstation for use with graphics only. The workstation may have several types of graphics software, several output devices (printers or plotters), high resolution monitor (enhanced graphics adapter EGA and EGA monitor), mouse, light pen (if needed and supported by the software), 35mm color slide preparer, and any other peripherals necessary to support graphic users. In this way the workstation may be used more effectively by several people rather than making the investment several times.

COMPUTER-AIDED DESIGN (CAD)

Computer aided design software is as similar to graphics software as Mt. Everest is to a small hill, but a mention of this fast growing use of microcomputers seems to be warranted at this point. As microcomputer hardware moves toward the power of the mainframe and minicomputers, software once dedicated to the computer mainframes is being written for the microcomputer, bringing this technology down in cost and making it available to the smaller organization. This technology is especially significant in the organization that depends on engineering and architectural design specialists and their tools. Computer aided design (CAD) packages are removing the need for drafting tables, T-squares, French curves, and mechanical drawing tools. A dedicated CAD mainframe or minisystem may cost as much as $50,000, but one that is microbased is priced significantly less.

The CAD package allows the user to make architectural or engineering drawings using the microcomputer keyboard, electronic mouse, or a digitizing slate (a kind of electronic blackboard) as input devices. Most well-designed CAD packages have predefined elements or canned pictures and will allow the user to choose, size, and modify these elements to meet specific needs. Moreover, the software should allow the design and saving of elements or pictures that are peculiar to the needs of the user.

If there is a need for a micro-CAD package, the manager should be aware that there may be a need for a specific hardware configuration. A hard disk and a micro with an 80286 or 80386 processor are almost mandatory for processing speed. A wide carriage plotter is necessary for professional blueprints.

Just as the pocket calculator made the slide rule an engineering dinosaur and the microcomputer similarly affected the pocket calculator, microbased CAD systems are having the same effect on more traditional blueprint preparation.

ELECTRONIC PUBLISHING

The microcomputer revolution has spawned another buzz word—electronic publishing—this time for a technology that replaces many typesetting jobs by in-house production, using a microcomputer, desktop publishing software, and a laser printer. This technology may also include just producing the typeset copy and still using the printer which has large volume printing output.

Just a short time ago letter quality word processing was the important role of the microcomputer. Now this new electronic publishing area is becoming more important for many companies, even if they do not publish materials.

This technology allows the company to produce near typeset work from their microcomputer. Often it includes other tools such as graphics software, word processing, scanning devices, and others as part of its technology. The purpose of all this is to produce high quality documents such as brochures, newsletters, price sheets, and other documents that need to appear permanent or provide a specific image. It will produce the documents with features such as column setting, cut and paste, and special edit features that make the production of certain types of documents possible.

It is true that many companies use just word processing systems to produce such documents; however, many documents demand many more features to be produced than are available in this type of software. Many of the microcomputer areas revolve around software as being the key. This area requires the close working relationship of the input devices, unique software processing, and typeset output abilities.

Publishing software goes way beyond word processing software in its command interface and how it can manipulate character lines, columns and whole pages.

Electronic publishing has become feasible and popular mainly because of the release of cost effective desktop publishing software and laser printers. A laser printer today may run the same as a letter quality printer of just a year or two ago. The hardware is just as important as the software here. The software is being improved to make special tasks easier.

Electronic publishing will be especially important to companies in the publishing business in the future. However it will also be important to all businesses to cost effectively improve the quality of their communications.

What Can Be Done

A list follows of some jobs that may now be done or that can be brought in-house.

Newsletters

Brochures

Documentation

Price lists

Policy manuals

Product manuals

Training materials

Official form letters

Mass mailings

Catalogs

Product or other bulletins

Various marketing documents

Even with this technology, there are many jobs that should go to the printer, who can do the work better, quicker, or cheaper. However, the electronic publishing will improve on the quality of company correspondence and become more important in time.

Types of Technology Evolved

Input

Scanning devices to read words or pictures

Keyboards

Mouse

Electric pen light

Most microcomputers can perform these functions, but Apple, with their Macintosh, made this area simpler. Due to the popularity of this technology, many software companies are releasing improved versions on IBM and compatibles as well as other micros.

Software

Desktop Publishing—May include word processing, graphics, columnary settings, and other settings—easy ways to move pieces of text around and cut and paste the document.

Word processing

Thesaurus

Graphics

Drawing software

Character setting such as bold face type

Examples of desktop publishing software

Pagemaker

Spellbinder

Front page

Click art

Output

Laser Printer—Currently the most popular are HP Laserjet for IBM and compatibles, and Apple Laser Writer Plus, normally used for the Macintosh.

Cartridges that provide for a variety of fonts to be printed.

The output is very important to this quality typing area. Type in microcomputers is normally performed with the number of dots per inch. The HP Laserjet prints more dots per inch than a letter quality printer, and a letter quality printer prints more than a nonletter quality. However, the laser printer is normally faster than all the others. Of course, there are more expensive printers that print faster and clearer than the normally used business laser printer.

Combining graphics and text along with improvements in printer hardware has developed this concept of desktop or computer assisted publishing. This segment of the software industry grew from $0 in 1983 to over hundreds of millions in 1985. Software packages have the ability to merge text, charts, tables, headlines, dual columns, and drawings into documents that can be printed in such a manner that the quality is almost indistinguishable from a typeset manuscript. The manuscript, whether one page or book length, can also be taken to professional typesetters or office printers for final copy rather than printing it in-house.

The current direction is for desktop publishing services to be provided by vendors who have a variety of hardware such as laserprinters, typesetters, slide preparers, text scanners (to scan text in hard copy and transfer it to magnetic media such as a floppy disk), file transfer units (to transfer files developed under one operating system to another operating system), along with popular desktop publishing software, all for rent and use on premises. Some of these vendors are providing electronic file transfer through telecommunications with an initial hook up charge along with additional cost per page or kilobyte transferred. This latter feature will allow the user to prepare a document, send it by modem, and receive a finished product without leaving the office. These methods save the expense of the laser printer or other printer. The major reasons for the interest are the control one can exercise over the product, the speed of delivery of the final product, and the lowered cost per page.

If, for example, the organization prepares booklets for internal use containing material that may change in part such as local, state, or federal income tax rates, the ability to revise and reprint the booklets at an effective price and with timely delivery is important. The firm that produces in house advertising or promotional literature, and other internally or externally distributed material may find desktop publishing software an appropriate investment.

10

PURCHASING AND IMPLEMENTATION CONSIDERATIONS

Purchasing and implementing microcomputer systems or add ons require the same care as in large systems, but within a much shorter time frame and at significantly less cost. The same type of analysis and controls should exist.

The steps should be:

I. Purchasing—Preinstallation review
   A. Needs Analysis
      Information requirements analysis
      Specific user needs analysis
      Future needs and usage analysis
   B. Software First
      Review of applicable software
   C. Hardware Next
      Review and analyze appropriate hardware and add ons
   D. Preliminary System Selection: Based on Steps A to C select two systems that may be appropriate and run tests on them in your specific environment.
   E. System selection
      Decide on the total system you will use.

II. Implementation

III. Postimplementation review

The above is a general approach. Chapter 8 describes a specific approach to accounting software. Chapter 5 describes specific considerations for a

DBMS package. The type of software and hardware to be installed will always require other factors to be considered.

Following is a reprint of an article by Harvey Shuster and Paul Warner in the NAA's *Management Accounting* magazine that discusses these issues:

MICROS FOR SMALL BUSINESS: THE TIME IS NOW

Waiting for lower prices and for stabilization of the computer industry may be very costly to companies which could be improving their performance with microcomputers right now.

Not long ago computers were used only by large businesses. Although computer service bureaus and time-sharing organizations served smaller businesses, they affected a very small portion of the internal operations of most of these businesses. In the large business environment, knowledgeable experts operated and controlled the computer; it wasn't necessary for business managers to understand computer concepts and ideology.

Both hardware and software companies have taken great strides forward in making the operation of a computer and the use of software as simple as possible. As easy as the operation has become, however, it is still totally dependent upon the people in the organization.

Nevertheless, the microcomputer is an essential tool in these times when inventories, accounts receivable, and company cash flow have to be well controlled. But, for the small business person, the choices and options often appear endless. For example, in addition to the many hardware companies concentrating solely on microcomputer manufacture, the mainframe companies, including giant IBM, now are producing microcomputers. Consequently, there is a vast array of hardware and software available, and this diversity blurs the distinctions between the good and the bad, the solid, well thought-out product and the ill-conceived and nonmaintained one. This is particularly true of software, which often is difficult to evaluate.

As a result, two of the most frequently asked questions are when and what. That is—When should I buy, and what should I buy?

The "when" is now! Microcomputers are becoming cheaper and more powerful, however, the productivity of the current models over manual processing will pay for itself in a very short time. The advantage of having a micro compared to having nothing far outweighs any potential cost reductions or near-term improvements in microtechnology. Instead, write off the computer over two or three years and then buy a newer model.

The "what" is dependent upon your specific needs and local support. When first starting off, keep it simple. This way you can have a small success instead of a large disaster. Keep the system flexible and expandable.

Microcomputers have the capability of revolutionizing small business bookkeeping. Information that was elusive and difficult to prepare can be made available at a touch of a few buttons. Table 1 provides examples of what most microcomputer software can do.

A PROPERLY DESIGNED ACCOUNTING SYSTEM

Merely computerizing an existing manual accounting system, however, will not achieve the benefits possible through these applications, unless the basic accounting system is properly designed and controlled. A good time to examine the total financial function is when you buy a computer. Buying computers just to do the basics is like getting a telephone that only can dial locally. It will do the job, but the true benefits that can be derived for the business are not realized. This is a time where the total accounting system should be reviewed. For example, with a microcomputer you can:

- Create a new chart of accounts to provide for segregation of significant cost centers. These centers could show what the costs are in each function of the company (e.g., sales department, shipping, and so on). It could segregate the profit and loss by product line. Separate product line statements would make it easier to identify the profitable products from the marginal products—and, thus, provide you with relevant and timely data for decision making.
- Design a perpetual inventory system using an inventory package. With such an inventory package, you can take better advantage of information and obtain greater inventory turnover and the corresponding cost reduction.
- Prepare budgets and cash projections. Software is available which can provide insights into your company by analyzing the various expenses in the profit and loss statement and determining how

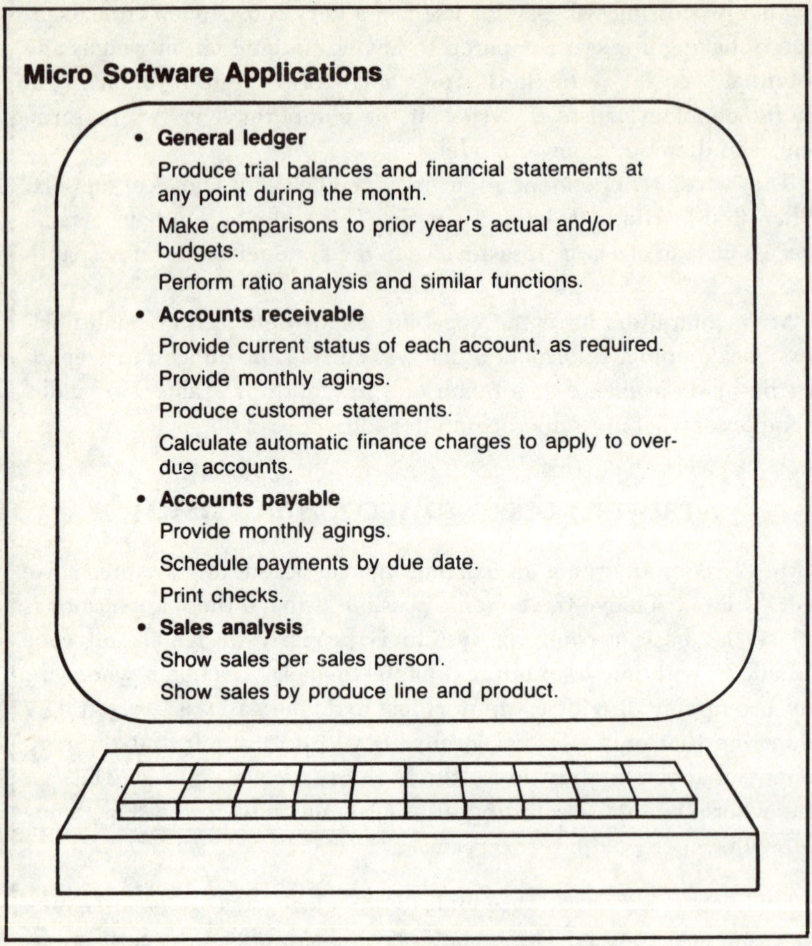

FIGURE 10–1 Microsoftware Applications

those expenses relate to sales. By projecting sales, you can determine the break-even point and the effect on the bottom line for various sales levels. This then can be used to monitor the availability and uses of cash.

MACRO REALITIES FOR SMALL BUSINESS

Software is the key to success for the small business that wants to take advantage of the microcomputer. Software produces the screen menus, stores the data in a particular order, and indicates to the machine how to print reports. It is the software that interacts with the user. There are many different ways in which you can create software. Some are costly; others are cost effective.

First, because microcomputers are moderately priced, software had to be developed which could be priced comparably. The cost of "off-the-shelf software" . . . ranges from a few hundred dollars to a few thousand dollars, office productivity software (word processing and electronic spreadsheets) being cheaper than accounting software. To keep software prices reasonable, therefore, it has been necessary to develop software in a standard manner for as many companies as possible. In this way, the cost of development can be spread among many users. Contrast this with the development of custom software for one company where that one company has to bear all of the development costs.

Also, software should be developed through the combined efforts of users, programmers, testers, technical writers, accountants, and so on. This way, the end result is not just a program, but a fully tested system, including essential items such as manuals, user instructions, and sample data bases.

Likewise, software must be installed properly and supported. It may not always fit the requirements of every environment, and there are always certain questions that must be asked to obtain its fullest benefits.

You should consider:

- How many accounts fit on a diskette?
- How many transactions can be entered?
- What is the account number range of the chart of accounts in general ledger?
- Does the G/L package have a flexible reporting system that meets your company's needs?
- Can the software be converted from diskette to hard disk because of changing transaction volume and speed requirements?
- Will a warning sign appear before running out of room on a diskette?
- Can I receive training on this package?

It is important that the developer offer a continued commitment to support the software, otherwise the software may be of little help for solving the particular business problems for which it was acquired. For example, a payroll package needs to prepare payroll in accordance with applicable federal and state laws. If the law changes, can and will the software be updated accordingly? This is an important requirement of quality software.

The value of the software is enhanced if it can be linked with other products. For example, accounts receivable should communicate automatically with the general ledger. Word-processing software also can be linked with the data files of financial accounting software. Beware of those companies that have a commitment to single product offerings because they may limit you in efforts to stay up to date with new software developments.

Another important factor is that the software selected shouldn't be locked into a specific brand of computer. Software can be designed to function under a universal operating system which operates on many different brands of hardware*. But don't assume that you automatically can move the software to another hardware brand; check first with the software vendor. *Some systems are: CP/M86 and MS-DOS. CP/M™ is a trademark of Digital Research, Inc. and MS-DOS™ is a trademark of Microsoft Corporation.

COMMON MISCONCEPTIONS

The proper selection, installation, and operation of a microcomputer system requires proper planning, including the elimination and/or replacement of poorly designed manual systems.

Two common misconceptions persist for many microcomputer users. One is the belief that microcomputers, because of their inexpensiveness, are extremely simple to integrate into a business and automatically will provide control of the business and answer all of its problems—including the elimination of poorly designed manual systems. The assumptions presuppose the capability of the microcomputer to be far above its actual capabilities. The other misconception is that microcomputers provide no cost benefits to the company. Neither is completely correct.

For example, the problems that have beset the large scale and minicomputer areas-where installations have broken down totally because of poor planning, disregard for running parallel (i.e., operating both the old and new systems until the new system is functioning satisfactorily), and other factors—could occur in the microcomputer area. More often than not this has occurred because medium-sized and smaller companies have acquired and installed minicomputers without obtaining guidance from independent accounting or computer professionals when the in-house skills were lacking. A frequent scenario is for an accountant to get a call such as, "Well, I bought one, I threw away my manual books, it doesn't work right, and now what do I do?"

Obviously, planning and professional help are as important in the microcomputer environment as in any other computer environment. Some of the steps necessary for the successful installation of a microcomputer system after a decision has been made to computerize with a microcomputer are:

Pre-Installation

- Examine the current system to obtain an understanding of how it works. Determine what changes should be made to obtain more accurate and timely financial information. Determine what controls are required. To computerize an unorganized, ill-controlled manual system could cause problems.
- After the basic financial accounting system is reviewed, determine what improvements should be made to obtain more meaningful management information. Analysis of product sales, cost accumulations, or budgeting should be used to control costs and monitor inventory requirements, and, possibly more important, to control cash requirements.
- Determine what software packages could be used best to computerize your accounting function. Then evaluate the available hardware that can operate the software. In addition, ascertain if training is available for your people.
- Bring the people who will operate the microcomputer into the planning process. It is much harder after they have said it could work for them to turn around and say it will not work. More systems have failed because of people problems than almost any other cause. The personnel who will operate the microcomputer must want to convert to a new system, be willing to learn to operate it, be able to adjust to change and be properly trained in its operation. Without a clear desire to change and modernize the

accounting process, the installation could be doomed. "User-comfortable" software should aid in this transition, and proper guidance and selection by a qualified accountant substantially improves the chances for success.

Software is the real key to small business microcomputer success.

Installation

- Prepare a plan for installing the hardware and software. The plan must include specific points at which the project will be reviewed.
- Install the packages one at a time. Normally, the easiest one should be installed first. Consideration should be given, however, to the package which will provide the greatest payoff, even though it may not be the easiest to install. The overall easiest package may be an electronic spreadsheet. The easiest accounting package may be accounts payable if the level of payables are small. Vendor files may need to be established but not a chart of accounts numbering scheme. If there is a significant receivable or inventory problem, maybe the installation of these packages will return the cost of the microcomputer soon after installation. An easy package, however, can spell success, and there is nothing better for a new user than immediate gratification through success, especially if this is the first computer experience.
- Provide sufficient time for training before installing any software. Formal training from one to three days per package and possibly an additional general familiarization may be needed based on the number of packages, complexity of software, and knowledge of computers. After this, use of the sample data which comes with the software is essential in order to obtain "hands-on" experience with the software.
- Where possible, use the revised manual accounting system for a period of time before using the computerized accounting methods or control techniques.
- Maintain the manual records for a period of months before discontinuing them. Parallel operation is critical. You must reconcile the old set of books to the new before switching over. The new system must come up with the same results or clearly definable differences.

- Always monitor the progress to determine if the installation is going as planned.

It is absolutely essential to have a concrete support commitment from every software provider.

Post Installation

- Always prepare back-up copies of your data disks. If the current disk is damaged, you can use another one that is fairly current. The back-up copies must be prepared at sufficiently frequent intervals to minimize the cost of reconstructing lost data.
- Prepare control totals of the data being input. Compare these totals to the computer printout and reconcile and control any differences.
- Independently determine the results of the processing. For example, in using an accounts payable system, compare your unpaid invoices file to the accounts payable aging.

MAKING IT WORK

The macro reality of the microcomputer is that it has modernized the age-old bookkeeping process. But software, the invisible instructions on the diskette, will be the main contributor to the small company's success in obtaining the true benefit from its microcomputer purchase. Small business operators may want to seek the advice and guidance of a CPA firm in applying this powerful new tool to the specific business, because by molding these tools properly to the specific environment, a greater return on these investments can be achieved. The microcomputer can become the tool for solving your accounting and planning problems as long as a systematic approach is taken in its acquisition, implementation, and operation. Proper guidance in its installation is critical to the successful use of a microcomputer in your company.

Reprinted from *Management Accounting*,
March 1984

Availability of a software vendor hotline is important. Be forewarned, however, that the existence of a hot line does not mean your troubles are over and all your questions will be answered. The support person is the key to a good user support system. Generally, support people are not familiar with the specific application and may be familiar only to a limited degree with the software package you are using. This may require the person to take your name and number and call you back after consulting with someone intimately familiar with the software. Moreover, hot lines have been notoriously cold when trying to get through for information. Busy signals are commonplace; therefore, if hot line support is important, call the hot line before you buy to determine the time of day it is least busy. Then hope that when you have a real question you can get through to the support person on the other end, and that person can answer you correctly the first time.

PART THREE

TOOLS THAT HELP YOU USE MICROCOMPUTERS

11

AIDS TO QUICK USAGE

In the mid-1970s, when microsoftware was first released, most developers believed the software consisted only of the program, and the line instructions written in a software language on a diskette. However, the microcomputer user was like no other computer user. On minicomputers and mainframes, dedicated resources and serious thought were applied before a purchase because of the equipment cost. Because micros were so comparatively cheap, a whole new user base (everybody) was created. However, everyone still expected the same quick usage and abilities at one-tenth the price.

TAILORED WRITTEN AIDS

To help the untrained user, work was begun on thorough, simplistic user manuals. Extensive work is continuing today on new user aids and training devices so the code is now only part of the microsoftware package that is delivered. No matter what the vendor can deliver, tailoring your own aids to your specific situation can significantly increase productivity. It can also significantly increase company control over the use the of the software.

An example of user aids that can come with a product are the ones that come with Symphony, the integrated office productivity package from Lotus Development Corporation. The aids included are:

Introduction booklet

How-to manual

Reference manual

Glossary booklet

Keyboard overlay for the function keys

Diskette case

Quick reference guide

Documentation and other materials supplied by the vendor can only go so far. In the beginning, however, the vendor's materials should be very useful.

PERSONNEL AID

A new type of person is being hired by companies to coordinate the use of microcomputers. Many times microcomputers are purchased by a department head and used for a specific departmental purpose, without regard to the company's data processing (DP) manager, the company's database of information, or what other software or hardware is used in other areas. This problem is leading to the proliferation of different software packages throughout the company, different types of microcomputers, and different databases of information. The facility coordinator, or other similarly titled position, is being added to corporations to coordinate the use of microcomputers.

They coordinate:

Where and how to use micros

Training of users

Evaluation and purchase of microcomputer related equipment and software

Modification of menus and programs

Support of all micro user questions from the secretary to the accounting department.

The person should coordinate with the following positions, if the company has them:

Chief operating officer

Chief financial officer

MIS director

Data processing manager

Information officer

This is important, because the microcomputer is becoming an integral part of companies' data processing and information gathering structures. For many years the microcomputer was seen as a stand-alone tool. The MIS director and data processing managers have been left out. This should not be allowed. Micros are being connected to minicomputers and mainframes. It is imperative that microcomputers be included as an integral part of the data processing function, in addition to being supported as a stand-alone tool. To coordinate these needs, the position of facility coordinator is being created by many companies.

These coordinators have crossed all company disciplines and all department lines. They work with everyone, from the clerk to the president.

In many cities, there are facility coordinator user groups that share common ideas, problems, and solutions.

MICROCOMPUTER INVENTORIES

Many companies have not coordinated any effort in the microcomputer area. Facility coordinators are starting to do this work. One of the first steps in gaining greater and better use of company microcomputers is to determine what is currently being used and available. It is surprising how much microsoftware and microhardware are sitting in the closet. To start the process an microcomputer inventory and survey should be prepared.

This will determine what is available, how it is being used, education levels of users, user needs, and many other items. It is surprising what will be found. One company found two computers in its closets. In addition, when management asked users if they were backing up disks, the users asked what that meant. The company immediately knew it had a problem.

From this step, integration of resources, training needs for users, and required company controls can be realistically established.

The list below indicates one example of a company micro inventory/survey.

Microcomputer Inventory and Survey

DEPT. NAME :

DEPT. HEAD :

DATE :

A. User Information

1. Position in company.
2. User training already received.
3. Experience with microcomputers
4. User problems and questions.
5. Person user calls if there are any questions
   a. Software
   b. Hardware
6. User educational requests
7. Additional microsoftware or hardware needed
8. Suggestions concerning microcomputer use

B. General System Questions

1. Uses of system
2. Estimate of time system is in use
3. People who are sharing system
4. Security and other controls over use
5. Logs that are maintained
   a. Usage log
   b. Software problem log
   c. Hardware problem log
   d. Repair log
   e. Back-up file log
6. System security procedures
7. Passwords or other controls detailed
8. Who purchases software, hardware, and supplies.

C. Information to Obtain

1. Back-up procedures of all systems
2. Print checkdisk of harddisk units
   At C: CHKDSK
3. Print directory and subdirectories of harddisk units
   At C: TREE
4. Print files on harddisk
   At C: DIR/W
   At all subdirectories same command and also for all disks
5. Print all template programs
6. Print other information from system

7. Warranty data

D. Microsoftware Inventory

1. Operating system
   Type
   Version
   Serial #
   Purchase date
   Purchase price
2. Application software following information for each
   Type
   Software
      packaged (company name)
      Modified
      Customized
   Integration to other packages
   Connections
      Networked
      Multi-user
      Micro-mini
      Micro-mainframe
   Application name
   Software developer
   Software distributor or dealer
   Version
   Serial #

Uses
Users
Periods data files are backed up
Where stored
Purchase date
Purchase price
Source code availability
Modification possibilities

2. Terminal
   a. Brand
   b. Model #
   c. Serial #
   d. Type
   e. Purchase Date
   f. Purchase Price
   g. Cables connected
3. CPU
   a. Brand
   b. Model #
   c. Serial #
   d. Type
      Single-user
      Multi-user
      Networked
      Other connections
   e. Internal memory
   f. Purchase date
   g. Purchase price
   h. Cables connected
   i. Drive type
      Floppy
      Hard disk
         Hard disk capacity
         Vendor if different from CPU

j. Boards
   Speed-up
   Graphics
   Expanded memory
   Mainframe connection
   Other

k. Maintenance contracts
   Vendor
   Period of contract
   Cost

F. Peripherals

1. Type
   a. Surge protector
   b. Mouse
   c. Bar code reader
   d. Other
2. Brand
3. Model #
4. Serial #
5. Purchase date
6. Purchase price
7. Purposes

G. Connections

1. Multi-user
2. Network
3. To mini
4. To mainframe
5. To external database
6. Purchase date and price of above

H. Security and Controls—describe security and controls in use not listed above.

In getting familiar with the software there should be no restrictions. Also, at this time not enough is known about the product usage to create your own material. Later, however, certain uses, concepts, restrictions, or aids that apply to your specific situation certainly could become necessary.

To provide added help in using the computer and its software you can prepare tailored aids beyond what the vendor can supply. Of course, much software does not come with aids from the vendor. Therefore, it is useful to prepare a general set of aids. Such aids might include:

1. Tailored reference cards
2. Micro user guide booklets
3. Tailored keyboard overlays

Computer information is only useful if you can get to it. That is why documentation is so important. After becoming familiar with the package, a user wants to operate the computer and perform commands without paging through the manual that is why reference cards can be a significant aid in operating the software and the computer.

With the explosion of software releases, many users are unable or unwilling to read extensive manuals. The number of different packages that are used places a burden on the user, who is not a computer-dedicated individual. Just as in the financial area where there are so many different financial standards (FASB's, APB's, SEC regulations, etc.), so it is in the microcomputer area.

A major frustration and concern of users is the inability to really take advantage of the computer software. Each package is different. Some operate in totally different ways than others. Special instructions are not needed to understand written information. However, the diskette presents a user media barrier, since you must know how to retrieve the information before you can use it. Many facilities are being developed to get past this problem, including help screens, documentation on diskette, and self-teaching tutorials.

Reference Cards

Reading documentation is important, however there are tools that help continued use and quick reference.

A reference card is a piece of paper someone can easily see, understand, and apply. It outlines commands, menus, or other functions of the software that are critical to its quick usage.

Reference cards are already included in many packages, especially the office productivity software. If they are not, creating one of your own could significantly simplify and make for more productive use of the software.

An example of where to use a reference card in accounting is the need for people just to use the query function. One of the microcomputer frustrations is the inability for someone to immediately obtain accounting information as compared to the manual system. (In both systems controls should exist over access.) A reference card can be created to show how to query the data. The access to the other menus and submenus can be restricted by use of passwords and other methods.

Documentation is for general usage and reference. It can be difficult to use as an active part day-to-day of operations because it is frequently large and has many different parts to it.

Reference cards provide numerous advantages. For example:

Daily use	Indicates procedures or steps to be remembered
Untrained user	Helps them use the software without extensive training
Sophisticated user	Lists commands or specific combinations of procedures or commands not in the documentation

Considerations for Developing a Reference Card

1. People and situations vary.
2. Specific problems or aspects may need to be considered.
3. There may be differences in:

   Uses of the software

   Number of users

   Specific instructions

   Importance of one part of the software to another

   Users' level of education

   Level of usage

The reference cards available with the software were created by the vendor for a general audience. The vendor generally does not have knowledge of the exact environment in which the software will be used. Even if a reference card comes with the software, creating your own special card which is tailored to the way you are using the software or to your specific problems is very helpful.

The tailored reference card does not have to be a long process and is fairly easy as long as you limit it to what you need. It is especially good if multiple software packages are involved. Even if the specific packages have cards, a combination of these cards into one card can simplify the overall usage of all the packages at your site. Checklists 11–1 to 11–7 show what, how, and where reference cards can be utilized.

Combining different software capabilities is important. That was the reason for creating integrated office productivity tools. Dunn & Bradstreet provides a service combining in one menu various software packages and external data bases. Internally produced, combined quick usage aids can deal with this problem also. Creating an overview menu, as shown in Figure 11–1, also produces ease of use.

Certain accounting software has a utility allowing you to create a new master menu that includes this vendor's software and any other vendor's software. Therefore, a new menu can be created to include the other office productivity software used. There are also utility packages that allow you to do this.
You can create this menu:
1. General ledger
2. Accounts receivable
3. Accounts payable
4. Accounts payable
5. Word processing
6. Electronic spreadsheet
7. Back up procedures

These new menus are becoming a requirement for periodic users of hard disk micros where each application is in a separate subdirectory.

FIGURE 11–1

CHECKLIST 11–1

Reference Cards Can Be Produced For

A. Types of application software

1. Office productivity—produced more for the specific commands, strings of commands, or other functions that help you run the software.

Software	*Ideas*
Electronic spreadsheet	Mathematical commands Macros to use or control the documentation; Cards for each function such as rate of return
Word processing	Commands—width, editing, printing
Project management	Entry, functional layout, and features.

2. Accounting software
   - Entry commands
   - Query commands
   - Index to manual
   - Parts of manual
   - Help facilities
   - Menu and submenu selections
   - Restrictions—dollar limits, volume of transactions allowed, or account number ranges
3. DBMS
   - Structure
   - Help
   - Functions
   - Limitations
   - Field availability

B. Operating software and utilities

1. Specific structure
2. Commands
3. Ways to use them

C. Computer operations

1. Turning on or off
2. Backup
3. Storage
4. Care
5. Control

Reference cards can be

a. A page or two of documentation
b. A three by five card with notes on it

c. Similar to a vendor reference card with extensive instructions and notes

Checklist 11-2

What a Reference Card Can Do

1. Serve as a quick reminder of essential commands that you use.
2. Serve as a quick reference for a string or combination of commands unique to your needs.
3. Index (just like a book) to find explanations of commands or procedures in documentation with page references.
4. Provide exact steps to produce a specific result like printing a report (allowing all authorized persons to get information off the diskette) without reading the documentation. They may not enter information, yet need to get to it quickly.
5. Aid those who do not use the software often and need reminders to get started.
6. Serve as a guide to steps not clearly explained in the documentation. For example, how to perform a series of steps, such as entering information then printing the transaction report.
7. Provide a list of menu and submenu selections available.

Checklist 11-3

Reference Card Possibilities for One or Multiple Software Packages on a Card

Of course each user has their own needs of what is useful to be on a reference card. The user who only queries information has totally different needs than one who enters data daily.

1. Operations of computer

   Start-up and turn-off instructions

   Operating system

   Company rules on activities such as backups and storage

   Necessary shutdown requirements

2. Software applications overview

    Software applications being used

    Start-up of software

    Menu and submenu selections available

    Function key or help facilities available

3. Specific function—detailed instructions to

    Enter information

    (If operators are locked out of changing master file)

    Train new operators

    Print out reports

    Perform month end, quarter end, year end, and related year end procedures

    Obtain query data

    Change report print-out structures

4. Specific companies detail steps to

    Turn on and turn off computer

    Operate software

    Operate hardware

    Indicate what can be stored on a hard disk

    Control use of application software

    Control who can use utility commands

    Use network system and who is indicated as responsible network controller.

    Includes step by step instruction for

    What key to push or what to type in

    What diskette to take in or out

    When and how to back up

5. Combinations of different software facilities that create one operator function, such as DOS commands for specific accounting functions. It becomes confusing if the software application does not mention basic commands outside of that software, as it is not part of their product.

    Operating software (DOS procedures)

    Utilities that work with application software

Backup

Move file

Format new diskette

Using new diskettes

All new diskettes must be formatted before receiving information, but this is a utility software function, not a part of the electronic spreadsheet or general ledger package.

6. Reference cards can act as an index—indexing all key software areas used. List various commands, functions, or instructions that may appear in a variety of software being used. The vendor's problem is not knowing all the software you are using.

   Your problem is assimilating and productively using all of the software. If you are using an accounts receivable package, electronic spreadsheet, and a word processing package, sections of a reference card could be:

   a. Turn on computer procedure
   b. Operating system commands
   c. Utilities commonly used
   d. Accounts receivable menus and commands
   e. Electronic spreadsheet commands commonly used
   f. Word processing
      Commonly used commands
      Commonly used functions
      How to use commands and functions
   g. Printing reports
      Accounts receivable system
      Electronic spreadsheet
      Word processing
   h. Transferring information from accounts receivable to the electronic spreadsheet
   i. Using hard disk and backup procedures

7. Entry of accounting software
   a. Turn on computer

b. Enter information for query

c. Print transaction report

d. Turn off computer

8. Overview of usage—accounting software

a. Available functions

b. Data entry formats

c. Date format

d. Turn on computer procedure

e. Password control

f. Entry routine

g. Turn off computer procedure

h. Commands on keyboard

i. Utility commands commonly used

Move file

Copy

Format

j. Dollar value limitations

9. Office productivity software

a. Turn on and turn off procedures

b. Frequently used commands

c. Frequently used commands outside of the software

Control-C key

Print screen keys

Space bar

Backup key

d. String of commands and formulas commonly used

10. Company created master menu screen.

Checklist 11–4

Using Reference Cards

1. Use it or change it so that you can

Place it next to the computer.

Tape a cardboard pocket to the side of the computer and keep the reference card in it.

Tape it to the wall so that you can see it when you are using the computer.

2. Make copies so that each person using the computer has access to a reference card.

3. Update card for clearer language so that it is more informative and more important items are indicated, also so buzzwords are eliminated.

4. Punch holes in one copy and put it in the user's manual to serve as a backup copy if others are lost.

Checklist 11–5

Preparing a Reference Card

A. Prepare for obvious uses

1. Use if there is an obvious problem or need.
2. Put on it as many recurring functions or problems as possible without making it too large.
3. Use clear delineations in the card if more than one application is being referenced.
4. Prepare for important items that are referenced frequently.
5. Use as a quick reference, not as a rewrite of the documentation.
6. Prepare especially if there are multiple software interfaces required to perform one user operation.
7. The reference card should not be more than six folded pages.

B. Use simple materials

1. Thick bond paper
2. Three by five card
3. Regular sheet of paper folded over three or four times
4. Adhesive backed paper that you can attach to the front of the computer

C. Organize

1. Label card.

    Type of reference card

    Software covered

    Applicable computers

    Name of person preparing it

    Applications

2. Date.

3. Organize materials into sections. Use short sections with numbering scheme, bullets in outline form, or indent.

4. Mark each section clearly.

5. Refer to the documentation when possible.

D. Keep it simple

1. Use simple language.

    Press key.

    Put diskette marked DOS in the disk drive instead of boot operating system.

2. Avoid computer jargon and initials if possible such as worm, system crash, or CPS.

3. Show exactly the name of the key or process. Instead of the word ENTER, use symbol press "gr05/k" if that is the key to be pressed to enter information.

4. Do not make assumptions, especially in this technical area where so much jargon is used.

E. Be precise

1. Show each step in a process if necessary for the level of user.

    Close door

    Push button

    Press key

    Type "GO"

2. Write down each word in the process. Clearly indicate what is an instruction from exact letters that must be typed.

Use quotation marks to indicate what must be typed.

Use figures to indicate what keys to press.

3. Clearly indicate the point at which to perform a step.

   At the A⟩

   At a submenu

4. Let someone else use the card to test it to make sure that it is correct.
5. Be consistent.

   In format

   In terms used

6. Be effective.

   Be sure to include instructions for unique or special information needed, actions performed, or special controls.

Each step in the preparation of a reference card may be modified and others added based on whether you are doing it just for yourself, your staff of two, or the accounting department of twenty.

CHECKLIST 11–6

Examples of Instructions That Can Be Misunderstood

1. "Copy the diskette." The person takes the diskette to the paper copying machine and makes a copy of it.
2. "Take the diskette out of the jacket." Instead of taking the diskette out of its paper holder, the person cuts open the square black plastic cover and takes out the round diskette. The paper holder was not shipped, so what was the person to do?
3. "Print report." The instructions never said to turn on the printer. The person did not know that the printer had a separate on and off switch.

The above are actual support calls that have been made to software vendors. Users are not dumb people. They are simply following the instructions exactly as they were written. Of course through training, users should be able to avoid these types of problems.

CHECKLIST 11–7

Variations for Preparing Your Reference Card

1. Underline or highlight with a marker an existing card
2. Use a page of documentation with your own notes
3. Take an existing card and make your own notes
4. Combine other cards into one card for your own use

NOTE: Remember, the vendor owns the materials that came with the software and they are usually copyrighted. You have paid only for the right to use them.

One method for formatting a reference card by columns:

Step	Type of step	Type or press	Instructions
Start up	Turn on computer	What key to use What to type in	Any additional notes needed on this step

12

CREATING YOUR OWN AIDS PLUS QUICK USAGE EXAMPLES

MICRO GUIDE BOOKLET

What we all could use is someone to help us find our way through the microcomputer jungle. Webster's New World Dictionary says, "A guide implies the showing of the way by one who is thoroughly familiar with the course, connotes his continuous presence or direction along the way." We all need a guide in using microcomputer software, especially in the beginning and if the software is used only occasionally. The guide can remind us again and again of the essential details needed to get an initial level of use from the software. The guide bridges the gap between looking at a blank screen and usage of the package. A micro guide booklet could be a 4 to 10 page document that aids the user in operating the software. It quickly gives the user specific instructions for the software and exact commands for the packages being used. Sometimes they come with the software; however, most times they are developed by the user.

Micro guide booklets differ from reference cards in that they are more extensive, provide greater detail on the operations, and are in booklet form. Many even give exact step by step instructions rather than just a brief list of commands. Most of the rules outlined for reference cards can also apply to micro guide booklets. The examples that follow may be reference cards or guides. The important consideration is the ability of the document to supply critical information without referring to large user's manuals.

Guides are not unique to the computer area. For example Dale Carnegie, the famous sales motivator, issued a 12-page booklet called How to Remember Names. This was a guide book also.

A booklet should be small enough to fit in a pocket. The following are examples of guide booklets:

Lotus's Symphony software has a Quick Reference Guide.

Peachtree Software's Peachtext 5000 uses a Quick Start Instructions booklet. It provides instructions for starting the word processing package, how to enter information, and how to print it without going to the documentation.

In concept and detail guides fall between reference cards and documentation. Guide booklets can be very effective in increasing productivity. They are also very effective tools, when tailored to a specific person or use.

An Example of Reference Card and Part of Guide Booklet

Turning on a computer

Getting into various software entry areas

Getting out of the software

Turning off computer

Guide booklets are a very effective way to combine company policies or controls with the operating procedures normally found in a user documentation. Some companies split them into two parts—Part I. Company Policies (see Chapter 13) and Part II. User Help.

Guide booklets and reference cards differ by length of the document, length of explanation, and presentation style. At times a reference card can be part of a guidebook.

Figures 12–1 to 12–5 provide different examples of reference cards and parts of guide books. (See pages 223–228.)

Prepared by: HS
Hardware: IBM/PC two disk drives
Software DOS 2.2[tm]
NOTE: This example assumes knowledge of how to use an IBM/PC

I. Commands

Function	What to type	Reference	Instruction
		IBM Guide to Operations supplied with IBM computer Chapter and page number	
1. Copy a diskette	A:Diskcopy	DOS 3–61 to 3–66	Never use original program diskette
2. Copy a file Named GO.WKS from A drive to B drive disk	A:Copy A:GO.WKS B:	DOS 3–71 to 3–77	In naming files use your initials, then description of work
3. Preparing a new diskette in drive B for information by formatting it	A:Format B:	DOS 3–52	WARNING—this command wipes out all information on the diskette. Some depts change name of Format command to another name for performing this function.
4. See a list of files on a disk displayed across screen	DIR/W	DOS 3–53 to 3–55	Print directory of your files weekly. Leave with V/P secretary.
5. Print information on screen	Press PrtSc key and shift key at the same time		
6. Stop information from scrolling on the screen	Press Ctrl and Num Lock key at the same time.	DOS 3-19	

FIGURE 12–1 Company Reference Card for Microcomputers

Program: Date MM/DD/YY
Electronic spreadsheet
repared by HS
Computer used: IBM/PC
Key—denoted by two disk drives

STEP	TYPE OF STEP	TYPE OR PRESS	INSTRUCTIONS
Start up	Turn on computers	Push red lever up on right rear side of computer	
	Turn on the printer	Press the printer on/off switch to turn on the printer	
	Start software	Put in diskette labelled DOS (in left hand disk drive door).	DOS diskette should have label side up. Put the notched end of the diskette in first.
		Push down disk door.	Cursor dash—appears in the left top corner of the screen. The red light on the left disk drive comes on.
	Date and time entry	Type the date in the format MM/DD/YY Example: Jan 2, 1985—01/02/85 Press the Enter Key. Type the time in the format 00:00:00. 00 (hour, minutes seconds, and hundreths of second.	Format examples: 1:30 a.m. — 1:30:00.00, 2:30 p.m. and 20 seconds—14:30:20.00 It is important to be sure you enter the date and time for future reference.
		Press the ENTER key.	At this point the "A:" appears.
Ready for software	Take DOS out and load Lotus	Open the left disk drive door Take out the DOS diskette. Put Lotus system diskette in left drive and close door. Put data diskette in right drive and close door. Type "LOTUS" press ENTER key.	

Press ENTER again. Then finally press ENTER once more for blank spreadsheet screen to appear.			
Using spreadsheet	Commands	Press / key.	A type of menu selection appears on top of the screen. On second line submenu selections are shown
Help	Press F1 key	Displays explanation of the specific commands shown.	
To end commands	Press ESC	System returns to previous menu selection, then out of commands selection	

WARNING: Never take diskette out of disk drive when red light on the drive is on or in the middle of a program or menu. Files on the data diskette could become disorganized. Make sure you go back to A: before shutting off the computer.

Save file		
Turning off at blank spreadsheet after saving it	Press / key	
Getting out of Lotus 1–2-3	Type Q for quit Type Y for yes Type E for exit Type Y for yes.	
Turning off the computer	Open the right disk drive door and take out the diskette.	Put it into the proper sleeve for storage.
		Open the left disk drive door and take out the Lotus system diskette. Push down the red lever on the right rear side of the computer. In back of printer press on/off switch.

FIGURE 12–2 Example of reference card with start up instructions and specific commands the user needs for Lotus 1-2-3.

Program: Wordstar[tm] (word processing)
01/15/85
Prepared by C. Wheeler
Reference card assumes that you know how to start the system and the software (Wordstar). It also assumes that you are using a two disk drive computer. It is not a complete list of Wordstar functions, only some of those the company personnel would commonly use.
At point where Wordstar Menu is appearing:

Activity	Instructions
Change logged drive	Press L to change the logged drive to the B drive. Then type B: and press ENTER. The B drive (the right side disk drive) is the drive to use for your data diskette.
Edit a file	Type D. If you are setting up a new file type the name you wish to use. Example: A letter to Mr. Smith—Smithltr could be an easily identifiable file name. Type the file name and press ENTER. To edit an old file, just type that file name and press ENTER.
Create a file	Margins are present at 1 and 65. If you want anything else, set them first. Also set spacing before you begin typing.
Saving a file	Kd—To save the current file and exit the file Ks—To save the current file and remain in the file Kq—To save the current file and exit it without saving changes made to the file
Exiting Wordstar	Type X to return to the system.

FIGURE 12–3 Reference Card

Prepared by: HS
Hardware IBM/PC two disk drives

A. Diskette Handling
    1. Do not bend
    2. Do not X ray
    3. Put sticker on diskette and label
    4. Use felt tip pen to write on diskette labels
    5. Store in paper sleeve
    6. Do not scratch
B. Warnings
    1. Do not operate computer when room temperature is over 90 degrees or leave on overnight or weekends when the office air conditioning is not operating.
    2. Use static mat
    3. Do not let unauthorized persons use production diskettes or machines.
C. Company computer policies

FIGURE 12–4 Start of Guidebook

1. Back up once a week
2. Store backups off site in a vault each month.
3. Computers on second floor available for all and can be checked out for home use over the weekend by the secretary.
4. All other computers are only to be used by authorized personnel on the operating list.
5. Password changed bimonthly.
6. Data diskettes to be locked in user's desk in diskette holder and production diskettes stored in locked cabinets, in diskette holder with rack.
7. Software library available on second floor.
8. All data diskettes with any financial information on them from accounting must have a protect tab on the diskettes. Use them for spreadsheets; however, do not change any of the original information.

FIGURE 12–4 Continued

Company's General Ledger

Entry of transactions:
Dates: Month day year
Format: mmddyy (format for entry)
Dates appear as mm/dd/yy after entry
Dollars: Enter 9999.99
Appears $9,999.99 after entry
Debits: No sign
Credits: Put—negative sign in front of the number
Help: Press H at any time for help facility
Enter General Ledger: Type Journal Ent and press
Transactions: ENTER to go directly to submenu.
Backup: Do daily
Store off site monthly

Menu Selection	*Documentation Page Reference Number*
File Maintenance	
Adding account	4–28
Deleting account	4–32
Changing account	4–34
Journal Entries	
New Transactions	5–2
Recurring entries	5–12
Adjusting entries	5–22
Query	
Query account history	6–10
Query transactions	6–20
By date	6–21
By journal entry type	6–23

FIGURE 12–5 Reference Card

Reports

Transaction report	7–5
Trial balance detail	7–10
Trial balance summary	7–12
Balance sheet	7–16
Operating statement	7–20
Funds statement	7–25
Cash flow statement	7–30
Budget report	7–35
Comparative report	7–40

NOTES:

1. Any submenu can be accessed by typing the submenu name.
2. Passwords have to be used for entry.
3. Different passwords used for maintenance.
4. Help facility available for complete documentation or a specific item.

User Notes:

____
____
____
____
____
____

FIGURE 12–5 Continued

KEYBOARD OVERLAYS

Keyboard overlays explain the functions of specific keys. Instead of trying to find the operation of a key in the manual, use a keyboard overlay on or next to the keyboard to speed up operations and increase usage of keys that were programmed to help. Keyboard overlays are frequently included in the office productivity software. Again, creating your own tailored keyboard overlay or a new one will speed up operations, and act as a reminder.

Examples of keyboard overlays:

1. Some software vendors supply keyboard overlays for their specific programs, such as Lotus 1-2-3 by Lotus Development Corporation.
2. Some companies offer general use keyboard overlays for sale as a separate product, such as PC-DOCUMATE™ by Systems Management Associates.

3. The user can prepare certain types of keyboard overlays.

They can be:

- A plastic unit that fits around a set of function keys that perform specific operations within the software
- A cardboard fitting around or on top of the keys
- A cardboard or other material placed near the computer
- Any type of easily visible key reference that is attached for immediate use

These aids can be prepared simply and easily if not supplied by the software vendor. Here are some ideas for preparing keyboard overlays:

- Make them small
- Attach them to an area that is immediately visible
  - Around keys
  - On top of keys
  - On bottom of keyboard
  - On terminal
- Use one or two-word instructions
  - Edit
  - Help
  - Print

Keyboard overlays assume knowledge of the computer and the software. They are very brief and direct. Figures 12–6 to 12–8 are examples of keyboard overlays.

F1 PRINT	FUNCTION KEYS	F6 INSERT
F2 EDIT	IN THE	F7 HELP
F3 ESCAPE	MIDDLE	F8 GO TO
F4 SCROLL		F9 DELETE
F5 SAVE		F10 LOAD

FIGURE 12–6 Overlay Around Function Keys Specific Software Commands (Not DOS Commands)

ESC	*Ctrl-C*		*PrtSc*
ESCAPE	STOP PROGRAM	ENTER	PRINT SCREEN

FIGURE 12–7 Overlay Placed On Top Of The Keyboard

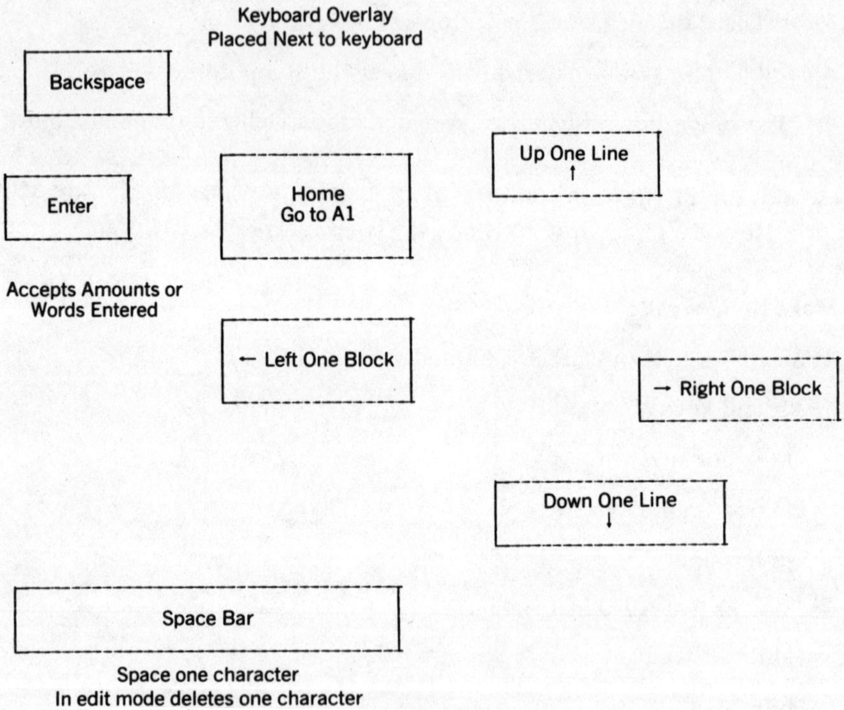

FIGURE 12–8 Keyboard Overlay Placed Next To Keyboard

13

YOUR OWN DOCUMENTATION

OVERVIEW

Written instructions (documentation to the micro user on operations of the system) have become as important as the software code itself. If no one knows how to operate the software it is totally useless.

The software vendor does not know exactly how you will be using the package so the documentation is written for all users. Obviously a word processing package is going to be used for word processing. However, in using it to prepare audit reports on SEC filings, additional instructions can be added that will increase the productivity of the package.

There are three ways outlined that can make these standard written instructions more applicable to your situation:

Tailored documentation—modifies the standard documentation for the way you use it—whether by specific reports, additional comments, or special routines.

Guidebook—small 10 to 15 page folder describing how to use basic features of the software quickly (see Chapter 12).

Policy manual—describes how user should apply software and sets company controls or standards around such usages.

Tailored Documentation

Tailored documentation is taking the documentation supplied by the software vendor and amending it to your specific usage or operating environment. You must be careful of the vendor's copyright in doing this. You cannot copy the vendor's manual. Call your dealer. Tailored documentation can make using the software:

Faster for specific uses

Easier to perform specific functions

Require less training to use more types of software at the same time.

It will allow:

Speedier processing

Quicker referencing

More detailed indexing

Additional specific instructions as they relate to the individual company

Clearer indication of specific sections of documentation for targeted usage

Checklists 13–1 to 13–3 and Table 13–1 provide details on tailored documentation and how to prepare them.

CHECKLIST 13–1

Ways to Prepare Tailored Documentation for Daily Operations

1. Take out of the user's manual the installation section and other start up instructions after software is installed, leaving only the instructions that are necessary for daily processing. The installation and start up instructions are needed only by a very few people.
2. Make handwritten notes concerning special routines, commands, or procedures that you use.
3. Pull out of the user's manual any parts of sections that could be used to create a small instruction book—report writing and inquiry instructions.
4. Add instruction pages in appropriate section of the manual.

5. Add to the user's manual a new section called Company Use. It could include:

    Forms for input

    Forms for conversion from manual to automated reconciliations

    Templates used

    Spreadsheets prepared

    Specific examples of reports used in the company instead of the sample reports included with the manual

    Required controls and ways to use the software

6. Annotate report section with specific reports and company needs.
7. Add schedule of reports and how often they are to be printed.

    Example: Accounts receivable

When to Print	Report Name
Daily	Transaction entry report
Weekly	Customer list
	Aging report
Monthly	All of the above
	End of month report

The tailored documentation does require using a large book, not a reference card.

CHECKLIST 13–2

The following is an example of tailored documentation for accounts receivable entry.

Add to documentation:
Company requirements and controls outside computer

Customer account number

First two numbers—the state

Enter daily

Reconciliation report completed daily for customer sales and cash receipts

Weekly reconciliation of input tapes to output transaction reports

Input form for customer transactions

Allowable entries to

Description column

Add inventory abbreviated description codes

TABLE 13–1 Examples of Tailored Documentation for Integrated Spreadsheets Audit Reports

Use	Package	Additional Items Placed in Manual
Audit workpapers	Electronic spreadsheet	Templates for worksheets. Forms used for Statistical analysis for specific accounts. Instructions on preparation depending on client: Manufacturers Service companies Banks Retail establishments
	Data base	Previous financials and/or other permanent information
	Telecommunications	Direction on who and exactly how to send financials to office responsible for consolidating financials
	Special instructions and reports	Relating to type of client Manufacturing Banking Service Retail Printouts to save describing specifically those functions needed
	Word processing	Confirmation letters; Other forms

TABLE 13–1 Continued

Use	Package	Additional Items Placed in Manual
	Audit software	Lead schedules and trial balance
Financial statements	Electronic spreadsheets or Audit (Trial Balance software)	Directions relating to worksheets for: Working trial balance spreadsheet Consolidating trial balance Balance sheet Statement of shareholders' equity Funds statement Comparative financial statement analysis Summary financial disclosures Description of formulas used
	Word processing or audit software	Footnote forms
	Graphics	Specific financial ratios and graphic disclosures of them
Audit report	Word processing or audit software	Types of audit reports

Checklist 13–3
How to Prepare Tailored Documentation

A. Provide organization
1. Organize within the current sections.
2. Organize in logical sections.
3. Provide detail index.
4. Number new pages appropriately.

B. Be all inclusive
1. Combine different packages so that you do not have 20 different manuals for 20 different packages.
2. Add, in appropriate place, specific operations concerning the computer being used. Using a floppy over a hard disk could certainly change the operating procedures.
3. Remember that you are responsible for the most effective use of the software. The software vendor cannot do this for you. For example, an accounting clerk could have a daily operations manual that in-

cluded instructions for accounts receivable and inventory entry procedures.

Because a company may use many different software packages, tailoring one manual that includes the relevant portions of many manuals for a specific operation could be very useful.

C. Provide overviews and flowcharts of the computer operations

1. The manual operations that affect computer usage are an integral part of what the software can do.

   Examples:

   An operator using a spreadsheet for sales analysis for various products, regions, or people needs to know what source documents to use and to whom it is distributed. Tailored documentation could include:

   Templates for sales analysis

   Source documents

   Verification procedure for source documents

   Distribution of the analyses

   Responsible reviewer or auditor of report

2. The procedural flow charts aid in understanding the total process. The flow charts should include all manual and automated procedures required to complete the process. Too often, the computer is thought of as an end all to the process. It is a tool to improve the process, not the process itself. Example: Sale order entry. Use flow charts of the process. In a sales order entry process, the documents and outside controls are very important. An operator's manual should include a flow chart of the total process. It should show process from the initial order call to the shipment of the goods, including the microcomputer processing that is in the middle of the total process.

D. Detail

1. Write all instructions in detail.
2. Do not abbreviate.
3. Include all reports the way they look.
4. Double space or leave enough room for it to be easily legible or for notes to be added later.
5. Include date prepared.
6. Include name of person who prepared it.

7. Provide detail of company specified codes and their usage.
8. Provide detail of specified company choices in master files or other critical areas.

E. Keep it simple

1. Use simple words.
2. Use specific words or terms easily understood in your company.
3. Separate by bullets.
4. Use two columns with the left column for the general description of what is being explained and the right column for the detailed instruction.
5. Use two columns with the left for the exact input into the computer and the right column for the explanation.
6. Keep it short.
7. Use a numbering scheme within the new documentation.

F. Be specific

1. Use terms that are automatically understood in your specific industry and company.
2. Include samples of all reports generated.
3. Include examples of the entry screens using specific company information.
4. List exact software and menu or submenu being referenced.
5. Refer to page number of the appropriate documentation.
6. Describe exact computer and any peripherals being used.

G. Follow other simple rules

1. Be clear.
2. Be precise.
3. Do not make assumptions.
4. Be consistent.
5. Make several small sections rather than a single large one.
6. Reference other materials available.

    Start up manuals

    Operating manuals

Computer manuals

Reference cards

Tutorials

Policy Manuals

Company policy manuals are becoming common. These policies are important especially in a large organization. A constant struggle exists between: Personal micro freedom and necessary corporate control and consistency.

The essence of personal computers is the opening of the data processing doors to everyone. However, in larger organizations the establishment of separate data bases, which produce different numbers to analyze, can affect decisions. Coordination of information and maintaining integrity of data is important while at the same time allowing freedom. A computer policy manual written to provide for this can go a long way in obtaining this match.

In computer operations a policy manual can provide:

1. Direction for usage
2. Controls over operations
3. Restrictions in access
4. List of freedoms available
5. Appropriate data bases to access
6. Password control

The company computer policy manual can have a two-fold purpose.

1. Help user apply applications consistent with corporate requirements
2. Control microcomputer usage in accordance with a specific company policy.

They normally indicate how the company wants the technology used and what actions are not allowable. Just as personnel policy manuals indicate employee benefits and rules, the company computer policy manual indicates the computer's benefits and rules for usage.

CHECKLIST 13–4

Policy Manual Items

1. Backup procedures
2. Access—see Table 13–2
3. Library of software available to be checked out or taken home
4. Computers allocated for:
   - Accounting operations with access only by authorized personnel
   - All operations
   - Home usage
5. Input sheets
6. Reconciliation forms
7. Operational flowcharts
8. Current computers
9. Current software
10. Current usage
11. Password control
12. Networking procedure
13. User training
14. Future plans
15. Ties to other office computers
16. Ties to outside data bases
17. Intercompany charges for usage
18. Required common controls outside the computer
19. No copying of vendor disks
20. Privacy of information

CHECKLIST 13–5

Computer policy manuals can take the form of

1. Complete binders of detailed descriptions

2. A few pages of overview
3. Reference card of specifics

They also can change due to changes in:

1. Size of organization
2. Utilization of software
3. Number of computers
4. Number of users
5. Controls desired
6. Other computers used
7. Ties to other computers at same location or other locations
8. Level of training provided

TABLE 13–2 Manual Section On Controls

Chart of Software Authorization

Date:
Prepared by:

Authorized Persons	Electronic Spreadsheet	Word Processing	External Data Base	Accounting Entry and Query
Senior Manager	X	X	X	X
Managers	X	X	X	
Secretaries	X	X		
Marketing	X		X	
Accounting	X	X	X	X
Entry personnel and supervisors	X			

Control for Authorization Codes:

14

ENHANCEMENTS

ADDING MORE POWER TO YOUR COMPUTER

The desire for higher levels of knowledge distinguishes the professional. In the microcomputer world additional knowledge is frequently a beneficial side effect of additional computer hardware and software and the skill to use them. The following are computer add-ons that prove useful to large number of computer users, listed in approximately the order most people purchase them. The order in which you wish to acquire them may be slightly different, and you should feel no obligation to have them all.

In adding anything to your system, especially hardware, you will find that in-depth knowledge is needed. If you are not personally knowledgeable in the specific systems involved, you will find that good advice from an internal consultant at your company, an outside consultant (CPA or other), or competent dealer will be very valuable. It is possible to buy almost anything by mail order, but the advice and support you get from knowledgeable people is worth much more than the slight difference in price.

If the knowledgeable person in question is a computer dealer, develop a good relationship with one who carries a wide variety of products, who has the ability and willingness to help you determine your needs, and who will let you try before you buy. As your system and your needs become more complex, there will be more chances for incompatibilities to crop up; a good advisor will be able to warn you if you are heading for trouble.

Hardware

The Computer. Get a good, solid microcomputer compatible with the software you need to solve your initial problem, but not a machine so specialized that it won't run any other programs. The usual base line business microcomputer will probably have floppy disk drives (two are required for most business packages), a moderate amount of memory (check the requirements of your software, or just say "fill 'er up," memory is relatively cheap), and a black-and-white (or green-and-black or amber-and-black, but in any case monochrome) monitor. If you want to see color graphics on the screen, start with a color graphics screen instead of a monochrome (although some monochrome systems can do excellent graphics), but remember that the quality and readability of text on most color screens is inferior to that of most monochrome screens.

The Printer. Select a printer capable of producing the reports your initial software package produces. A dot matrix printer normally should suffice unless you will use word processing heavily. Even dot matrix printers can produce surprisingly good, readable text, albeit at a reduced speed, so plan to look at several before choosing. Dot matrix, laser image, or ink jet printers have amazing flexibility of type styles, making reports possible in formats not available on letter quality impact printers.

The printer should be capable of handling full sized computer paper (15 inches wide), and compressed print (usually 16 or so characters to the horizontal inch) is a necessity if you will be doing spreadsheets. Also, printers are rated in characters per second (CPS) or lines per minute (LPM) rather than words per minute. The LPM is a bit arbitrary, since the width of a line varies, but most often refers to lines of 132 characters, the width of most data processing reports. Both CPS and LPM figures vary even for printers of the same actual throughput, because different manufacturers have different ways of measuring speed. Text density has a major effect on measured throughput. Text with a lot of spaces and blank lines can be printed much faster, in LPM, than text that consists mainly of actual letters. In addition, printers vary in the speed at which they move the paper when not printing, as well as the logical and physical mechanisms that locate the printing element. The result is that printers with identical CPS and LPM ratings may have significantly different actual production speeds. Have someone familiar with different printers show you the difference.

The following comparisons of sustained speeds may prove interesting:

Device	Speed Range		
Human typist	60 WPM	6 CPS	3 LPM
Superhuman typist	120 WPM	12 CPS	6 LPM
Slow letter quality printer	200 WPM	20 CPS	10 LPM
Letter quality printer	550 WPM	55 CPS	27 LPM
Slow dot matrix	600 WPM	60 CPS	30 LPM
Medium speed dot matrix	1500 WPM	150 CPS	75 LPM
Desk top laser printer	2000 WPM	200 CPS	100 LPM
Fast dot matrix printer	6000 WPM	600 CPS	150 LPM
Mainframe report printer	48000 WPM	4800 CPS	1200 LPM

(These numbers could vary)

Enclosure. If the noise of the printer is too much for you (and for dot matrix or letter quality impact printers it may be), consider the purchase of an acoustic enclosure to muffle the sound.

Laser Printers. Laser printers use a technology similar to that used by a copier; they can print many different type styles and graphic images on the same paper and do it at a rate of about six to ten pages a minute. Unfortunately, they usually will accommodate only letter and legal size paper, not 15 inch computer paper, and require special software to produce most of their tricks. The trick you will want most often is to be able to print wide spreadsheets; so choose a laser printer that your software can drive in landscape mode that is usually over 200 characters per line on letter sized paper. Of course you can compress print the numbers and letters so many large spreadsheets can be printed on small paper.

Graphics. If the primary program you wish to run will produce graphic images on a laser or dot matrix printer, be sure the printer you select is one the program can use. Printers differ in their ability to do graphics, and every program will not work with every printer. Make sure your software will produce the results you want run on your type of computer using your type of printer.

Memory and Clocks. The most frequent first hardware add-on is more memory for the computer. Current software, especially spreadsheets, are memory hogs, and the amount of data you can manipulate is dependent on the amount of random access memory (RAM) in the computer. RAM is not to be confused with disk capacity. Popular business computers similar to the IBM PC and derivatives can use up to 640k (640 times 1024) of RAM.

Some computers require that add in memory of this type be mounted on additional circuit boards, and frequently these boards have other accessory circuits on them. Frequently, found accessory circuits are a clock/calendar or a serial communications port. The clock/calendar and attendant software will supply the time and date to the computer when you start it, so you needn't do so. The serial port can be used to connect a modem.

Extended Memory. Some computers can accommodate up to 2 megabytes (more than two billion characters) of RAM memory, but the software and the extra memory must both be designed for each other as well as for the computer in question. The specifications and process in this area are changing quickly, too quickly for a book like this one to give you the latest information. Ask your consultant for the latest specifications on which programs and memory schemes work together.

Date and Time. Many computers have the ability to date and time stamp the files they store, recording the date and time the file was last changed. This is invaluable in tracking changes made to various files, and solves the question of the currency of a specific version of a file. Naturally, if the computer is not equipped with its own internal clock (with a battery backup so the clock runs even when the computer is off) it will ask you the date and time when you turn it on. Always supply this information, or you will not be able to trust the dates and times assigned to your files. A clock/calendar board will obviate your having to supply this information each time you start the computer.

Hard Disks. If your computer is not already equipped with a hard disk, you will find the extra convenience of this item worth the price. A hard disk unit is a data storage unit similar to a floppy disk in drive. The capacity of floppy disks is measured in kilobytes (1k is 1024 or 2 raised to the tenth power), and a commonly found capacity for floppy disks is 360k. Hard disks' capacities are measured in megabytes (1M is 1,048,576 or 1024 times 1024).

A frequently found hard disk capacity is 30M, or about 90 times as large as a 360k floppy disk.

Or course there are 10M and 20M hard disks. Hard disks are available for most business computers, as either internally mounted units, or as external expansion units in separate boxes. On some computers there is a performance advantage to the internal version, so inquire before buying.

Because hard disks store more information, backup procedures must be faithfully followed and extra care must be taken to prevent software package A from damaging the files of software package B, something you needn't worry about when the software and files are on separate floppy disks. Another hard disk consideration is that of software copy protection: Some software cannot be installed on hard disks or if installed, require the floppy disk to be in a drive before they will work. This is another area for specific recommendations from an expert. Also all of the information is on the hard disk compared to a diskette that can be locked up. Additional access controls should exist on these systems.

Other Disks. There are also removable media disks of greater capacity than floppy disks; as much as 20 megabytes.

Disk Capacity. Both the kilobyte and the megabyte are rather strange numbers because they are computed in the binary (base 2) number system used inside computers. You don't need to know binary math to buy a hard disk system,since your dealer will take decimal (base 10) money.

Tape Backup. Microcomputers can use special tape cartridges to make backup copies of the information on a hard disk. Although tape backup is much quicker than making backups to multiple floppy disks, there is the question of cost. In general, tape backup seems more suited to someone who has a great deal of important information that changes often (i.e., accounting records) than to someone who has a lot of archival information that changes infrequently (word processing or spreadsheets). Floppy disks work well for incremental backup (copying only that which has changed), but not too well for whole disk backups, which are better handled by a tape unit. There are programs that significantly speed up this back up process.

Modems. Modems transform data into special tones that can be sent over normal telephone circuits. A modem can be used, with appropriate software, to connect your microcomputer to another microcomputer or to a mainframe computer so that information may be exchanged. Please see Chapter 7 on telecommunications for a complete discussion of modems, telecommunications software, and information utility services.

Color Graphics. If the software you use must have the capability of displaying color graphics and you need to see color graphics, get a color graphics setup. It won't be cheap and, in general, most color graphics setups have text characters that are a little hard to read; but if you want to see multicolor pie charts on your screen you have no choice.

Some computers will do graphics but not color graphics on their regular monochrome screens. The graphics display will use shades of gray or green to represent the range of colors. Many of these computers will require only a color monitor to do color graphics, saving you the price of the color graphics adapter card.

Some computers will allow you to have both a monochrome and a color screen in the system at the same time and show different displays on each.

Plotter If you need color graphics on paper you will be in the market for one of these devices. Compatibility problems abound in this area so you must again seek good advice.

Beyond this point most business computer users are into the realm of specialized hardware applicable to their specific business. As microcomputers become more powerful and users' expectations grow there will be more add-ons than a book this size could catalog. The devices you may add can be separated into three categories:

1. Input devices
2. Output devices
3. Other devices internal to the computer

Of course, one or more of these types of devices may be combined into a single unit to provide a special function. Input devices available at this writing include

Keyboards
Modems
Mice
Special keyboards and numeric keypads
Optical character readers (OCR)
Bar code readers
Foot-operated cursor positioning devices
Graphic digitizing pads
Touch pads
Speech digitizers and input devices
Joysticks, trackballs, and other game devices
Television cameras

Output devices available include:

Letter quality impact printers

Laser printers

Ink jet printers

Dot matrix impact printers, color printers (dot matrix and ink jet)

Modems

Voice synthesizers

Numerous types of special printers and plotters

Special graphics displays

Photographic slide cameras

Internal computer devices include:

Telephone interfaces and dialers

Analog to digital converters for data acquisition

Video disk interfaces

Backup tape units

Hard disk units with removable disks

A Word about Mice

A mouse is a small device attached by a wire to a computer. Moving the mouse across your table can, if the software you are using accommodates mice, move the cursor around on your screen or perform other tasks. In order to use a mouse to its best effect, a program must be written to accommodate it; however, many business programs were designed before mice came into vogue. To use a mouse to position the cursor on the screen requires that you remove your hand from the keyboard, which many experienced operators consider a bother. Worse still, a mouse requires a clear area on your desk, so the mouse can be moved around, and clear desk space near a computer is a rare commodity. Nonetheless, many computers are built around the idea of pointing to a command rather than typing it, and an increasing amount of software is available that will use a mouse at least as a cursor movement device. It is, of course, your call, and a clear try-before-you-buy decision.

YOUR SOFTWARE LIBRARY

Software is the fuel for the personal computer system. Without software the computer is clearly inferior to a toaster as a solution for business problems; at least the toaster can help make breakfast. Software is also the most personal and job dependent part of the system. Expect to spend more time picking software than you do choosing hardware, by a ratio of two to one or more. In fact, choose the software first! Choose the software that will solve your problems your way, then buy the hardware necessary to run that software.

Too many times the hardware is purchased first, then everyone runs around and tries to find out how to use it.

Summary Software Library

Spreadsheet. As a financial professional your first software acquisition will probably be a spreadsheet or an integrated package based on a spreadsheet. The important things to consider here are the size of your computer, the memory requirements of the software, and the size of the worksheets you will be calculating. As always, buy as much capacity as you can, since you will eventually exceed whatever capacity you have.

Most dealers offer training courses for this most important type of software. Don't be hesitant about attending the sessions since most of your fellow students will be businesspeople, too.

Examples.
1-2-3 (Lotus Development Corp.)
Multiplan (Microsoft)
Supercalc 3 (Sorcim/IUS Software)
Framework (Ashton-Tate)
Symphony (Lotus Development Corp.)
Jazz (Lotus Development Corp.)
Excell (Microsoft)

Text Editor. Even if you will never do any word processing, get a good text editor or word processor that will handle straight ASCII files. Question your vendor closely on this point, since one of the functions of this editor will be to touch up worksheets printed to disk by the spreadsheet program, and to edit information captured from the information and news utilities (the Source, Compuserve, Dow Jones News/Retrieval, VU/TEXT, etc.) via the telephone. In either case the text editor must be capable of manipulating text without converting it to some proprietary format, and many full featured word processors store their files in proprietary, non-ASCII formats.

Examples.

PMate (Phoenix Software Associates)
WordStar (MicroPro International Corp.)
PeachText (Peachtree Software, Inc.)
Word Perfect (SSI)

Special Printing.

If the spreadsheets you produce are wider than your software and the printer will handle without breaking lines, there are programs that will rotate a spreadsheet 90 degrees and print it sideways on the printer. These programs are considered utilities in many offices. They are cheap and will save you a fortune in Scotch brand tape. They only work on dot matrix printers.

Example.

Sideways (Funk Software)

List manager.

If you have lists of things, you need a list manager or small data base manager. This type of software lets you organize data and reorder it to suit your immediate needs. The lists can contain customers, prices, addresses, real estate listings, sales invoice records, or other information. Some DBMS programs also contain a calendar manager or datebook, and if the hardware is capable of it, dial your telephone.

Remember when choosing a list manager or data base package that you will probably have relatively few (by data processing standards) items on each list, so massive capacity is not necessary, but speed and ease of use are.

Some of the integrated spreadsheet software packages have some form of data base built in, so look at that part of your existing software before expanding in this direction.

Example. Mailing List Manager (Peachtree Software, Inc.)
Reflex (Borland International)
Habadex (HABA Software)

Communications. If you need to communicate with one of the information utilities (the Source, Compuserve, Dow Jones News/Retrieval, VU/TEXT, etc.) you will need telecommunications software in addition to the modem hardware. See Chapter 7 for a more extensive discussion of this subject.

Example. Crosstalk (Microstuf, Inc.)
Smartcom (Hayes Microcomputer)

Accounting Software

General Ledger. This will summarize all your postings and provide continuous and almost instant management reporting. For large corporations able to use the microcomputer, certain packages are written for the large dollar amounts involved and incorporate sophisticated report writers.

Other Accounting. Accounts receivable, accounts payable, fixed assets, payroll, tax reporting. Other accounting packages even for certain large companies automate specific functions effectively. Many offer special programs (even the largest company can be considered) that deal with specific accounting areas not previously possible to be dealt with on a large computer.

Industry Specific.	Other accounting packages such as property management could certainly be part of a library of software.
Other Software	As useful

THE NEXT STEP

If you have these important building blocks, and any other software specific to your field, the next step is either to become a programmer or befriend one. In addition to the regular commercial software distributed through normal retail channels, there is a wealth of free, public domain software available. However, you will need guidance in selecting and using it, and a little help in finding it.

The same guidance will be necessary to make the most of the computer's operating system and its utility programs. It may be worth it for you to pay a good programmer or consultant for a few hours a month for the first few months you use your computer. The instruction you can get for your money will save you both time and frustration in the long run. Most programmers and consultants have developed their own libraries of programs to deal with common problems, and there is no reason to spend your time puzzling out a solution when the answer can be had for a few dollars. The programmer should not attempt modifications to packaged software unless you and the programmer are willing to assume all responsibility for the result. Few software authors or publishers will support their software if it has been modified and some prohibit modification completely. Instead, the programmer can help you organize your programs and data, improve interprogram communications, translate data from one program's format to another, set up backup procedures, show you shortcuts that speed up your work, and help with software and hardware installation.

ON PURCHASING A COMPUTER

When you have chosen the software you need to solve your problem and are ready to purchase your computer, you will be faced with a large array of choices, both in the machine to buy and the way to buy it. Laying aside the question of buying or leasing, there are still questions you will have to answer in order to get the right machine for the right price.

Since it is very difficult to forecast one's future needs and what forms those needs may take, one primary question concerns the flexibility of the computer's design. If it is flexible, how flexible is it?

One answer lies in the design of the computer. Some computers have space for additional or replacement electronic modules. These modules can provide additional functionality, and certain modules might be required by a particular software package. These modules are also called cards or boards; in either case they are a printed circuit board with a number of integrated circuit chips and other electronic components installed on them.

These add-in modules fit in slots in a bus. The bus is the group of parallel electronic pathways that connects various modules of the computer, and a slot is simply a place to plug one of the modules into the bus. These modules are typically memory modules, disk drive controllers, video display controllers, and serial or parallel connections for printers and other external devices.

In general, business computers and the more powerful home computers can be divided this way:

Bus oriented	IBM Personal computers (PC, XT, AT, and desk-top variants) Most IBM-PC compatible desktop and larger portables (AT&T, Compaq, et al.) S-100 business machines (about 40 manufacturers, almost all using the CP/M operating system or derivatives. Apple II and derivatives except IIc
Semibus	Tandy models II, 12, 16 and derivatives IBM-PCjr (substantially different from PC) Some IBM-PC compatible lap-tops
Nonbus	Apple Macintosh and derivatives Apple IIc
Bus computers	One of the advantages of a bus oriented system is that you will generally have a wider selection of types of add-on modules, a choice of suppliers for the individual modules required to make up your computer and a variety of suppliers, usually resulting in lower prices.

There are many bus designs and many suppliers making modules for these business computers. The most popular business computers are built around an open bus, one whose specifications are published and are supported by several manufacturers.

Semibus computer — Some other brands of computers are semibus-oriented, in that there is room for expansion but the bus design is proprietary to the manufacturer and may have limited third party support. Semibus machines have less flexibility than bus machines but may still have enough to do the job you want to do.

Nonbus computer — These machines are, from a hardware standpoint, less flexible, but generally have already installed in them all the functionality of which they are capable. Some of these machines provide connectors to which an expansion chassis may be connected providing some expansion capabilities, although usually these expansion devices operate at a slower speed than devices connected directly to the bus.

When purchasing a semibus or nonbus machine, be sure that it will do everything you want it to do since expansion is very difficult, particularly with nonbus machines. Even a memory expansion in a nonbus machine can be very expensive and may be impossible. Bus-oriented machines, on the other had, present you with a very wide range of choices. You can buy the box and have it filled the way you wish.

For example, let us consider the IBM Personal Computer XT (the Apple bus machines or an S-100 bus machine would follow the same pattern). It is possible to buy an IBM-PC XT with all IBM parts, or with a substantial number of aftermarket supplier parts; even the all-IBM version may be assembled at the computer store to fit your needs.

The computer dealer can buy IBM PC XTs with a minimum amount of memory (usually 64 or 128 k), one disk drive, and no video display controller. Many dealers do this and then build each computer to the customer's requirements, using a mixture of IBM and non-IBM parts. Thus it is possible to have a computer with an IBM label and motherboard (the large board the rest of the computer boards plug into) and nothing else. It is the 1980s equivalent of the 1950s hot rod.

The following list indicates the types of boards available for bus-oriented machines like the IBM PC, PC XT, or PC AT; all are available from a number of suppliers with the usual variations in price, performance, and reliability.

1. Memory (RAM)
2. Clock and calendar
3. Serial interface (RS-232 port)
4. Floppy disk drive controller
5. Hard disk drive controller
6. Video display adapter: monochrome, color, color graphics, high resolution graphics, or a combination of these
7. Parallel interface (parallel port, usually for the printer)
8. Modem
9. IBM 327x display terminal emulator
10. External device interface for fixed/removable disks, tape drives, or other expansion devices
11. High speed processor (CPU) or coprocessor
12. Local Area Network (LAN) interface

In addition, multifunction cards are available that combine the functions of several of these cards onto one physical card. One popular card combines additional RAM, a clock/calendar, a serial port, and a parallel port on a single card. A wide variety of other combinations is available.

Of course, floppy disk drives, hard disk drives, video monitors, keyboards, and terminals are all available from independent suppliers.

Unless you intend to become an expert on the possible configurations available for the computer of your choice, find a dealer or consultant and work with him in determining the best way to build the computer that will be best for your needs.

Most computer dealers will, if asked, provide quotes on all brand-name as well as hybrid computers; the difference in price for functionally equivalent units may be as much as 30 percent. On most brands, there will be no difference in service, and many independent vendors offer on-site maintenance contracts for hybrids.

Portable Computers

Many manufacturers make machines that are portable, meaning that the computer may be easily moved from place to place. Even a large, powerful desktop micro is quite portable compared to a mini or a mainframe, but some micros are designed to be moved as part of their normal working life. Portables are sometimes further divided into lugables and lap top. The lap tops are briefcase size or smaller, and the lugables are about the size and weight of a portable sewing machine.

In either case, if the portable is to be your only machine, choose it as you would any other microcomputer; if it is a road machine that will complement your desk top machine, pay careful attention to compatibility between the two.

Networks

Networks come in many flavors, and the exact use of the word depends upon the size of the computers being discussed and the people discussing them. Mainframe and minicomputer people think of networks as being distributed over wide areas, say east of the Mississippi, and connecting many computers of different sizes together for corporate purposes. Microcomputer people when they think network generally think of a local area network (LAN), a much smaller scale interconnection of computers.

LANs are possibly the most widely discussed microcomputer topic of the present day. Everyone wants one even if they don't know exactly know what one is.

LAN Magazine's Glossary of LAN terms defines a LAN as "A data communications network spanning a limited geographical area, a few miles at most." Most LANs are, in fact, smaller than that, serving one or two dozen users in a small company or a corporate department. Establishing a LAN creates a much more complex level of computer operation compared to the single micro sitting on a disk. The installation and operation should be structured similar to a minicomputer environment.

LAN Benefits

Although there are several types of LANs and several interconnection philosophies, the main task of the LAN is always the same: to allow users to share data and peripherals and to transmit messages from one workstation to another.

Of course, a small number of users can share data and peripherals simply by saving their data on floppy disks and walking down the hall, usually to see the software wizard or the guy with the super laser printer in his office. This scheme, usually referred to as AnkleNet, is certainly cheap, if not highly efficient. It is perhaps the most efficient, since people resist the trip unless it is really necessary, rather than using the make-three-copies-before-destroying-the-original philosophy engendered by too easy access to high speed labor saving devices.

LAN Security

In this discussion there is, of course, much talk of access; almost every LAN has some provision for limiting the access each individual user has to the data files and peripherals. An administrator of the LAN should be appointed. Generally, there is a log on sequence that must be followed each time a user wishes to gain access to the network, and the identification codes used in the log on are themselves controlled by the network administrator. The administrator may also be called the supervisor or superuser or some such. Controlling access is important to provide security for sensitive data files, and to prevent tampering by unauthorized persons or disgruntled employees.

Some LANs provide security on a file by file basis, some on a disk by disk basis, and some on other schemes. In addition, the security may be exclusionary (i.e., you have access unless specifically barred) or inclusionary (i.e., you must be authorized to use specific files, disks, etc., and may use no others).

Most LANs also provide different classes of access (read data only, read and write but cannot create, do anything but delete, etc.). This is a very broad subject, but should be an item of interest to any potential LAN buyers. Don't be afraid to ask your vendor.

LAN Types

There are three general types of LANs: those that have a single central server, which is a separate unit, (file server, printer server, communications server) for each task, those that can accommodate multiple central servers, and those that have no central servers at all, allowing every workstation access to files on all the other workstations.

Single Central:	Most LANs are of this type or can be configured this way. A large central disk or disks, a couple of printers (one fast, one letter quality), and the central network OS software are part of one central installation. Although the individual workstations may have hard disks, printers, modems, and so forth, the central unit or units are the focus of network activity. Some LANs allow one computer to be both a workstation and a server, but any data that is to be shared must be on the central disk, since workstation A cannot have access to files physically on workstation B, unless either A or B is a combination workstation/server.
Multiple Central:	Some LANs can be configured this way. Several computers or purpose built file server hardware units share the file and printer server tasks; they may be physically in the same closet, but they are logically separate units and may be located wherever necessary. The individual workstations may still have hard disks, printers, modems, and so on. Still, any data that is to be shared must be on the central disk, since workstation A cannot have access to files physically on workstation B unless either A or B is a combination server/workstation.
Multiple Distributed:	Every workstation can be server under this scheme, allowing controlled access to every file physically present on the net, if desired.

Of course, under any of these schemes, if a computer is both a workstation and a server, some performance degradation must be expected, just as general network speed decreases as more activity takes place. A single file server unit clearly avoids a number of problems.

LAN Hardware

LANs consist of computers and similar devices connected by a transmission medium, usually cable or other types of wire. It is important to consider the way a LAN is physically constructed, because as the size of the LAN grows (and it will) the costs of network boards and cabling can outweigh the money saved by sharing expensive peripherals.

Things to consider when comparing the costs of different networks:

- Network server software costs
- Network server hardware costs
- Per-workstation software fee
- Workstation network hardware costs
- Cost of special devices to connect printers, and so on
- Cabling costs:
  - Wire costs
  - Labor costs
  - Local fire code or building regulations—having to put network cabling in conduit within the ceiling or wall, can raise costs substantially
- Some networks require special junction devices where each station connects to the main wire
- Some networks require signal boosters if the main wire exceeds a certain length

LAN Logical Devices

LANs have three types of logical devices attached to them:

- Servers
- Workstations
- Peripherals

Let us, however, consider the three types of devices separately for a moment:

SERVERS: A server is simply a central physical device that takes care of storage, printing, or other activities that are common to all users on the LAN. File storage is provided on a file server, printing is controlled by a print server, external dial up communications are provided by a communications server, and so on. One physical box, of course, may be more than one kind of server. Some LANs allow more than one file server, and some allow workstations to be file servers as well.

WORKSTATION: The workstation is usually just an ordinary microcomputer with the addition of a network board and special software. This allows it to be connected to the network medium (usually a cable or other wire) and therefore to store information on file servers and use peripherals connected to the network.

On most LANs, a workstation can store its files on the file server and print its output on the LAN printer just as if those devices were physically part of the workstation. All the security and organization is taken care of by the network software. Some LANs can have many file servers and printers, and on those larger LANs, each workstation user must be sure to specify which printer or disk he wishes to use unless the network software has the ability to specify a default device.

PERIPHERALS: The peripheral most LAN users want to share is an expensive but infrequently used printer or plotter. Most LANs have print servers or print server software in the file server to make this possible. One $5,000 super laser printer becomes an good investment when it can be shared by 30 people on one network. Most LANs will allow a workstation to have a local printer as well as have access to the network printer(s).

In addition, most LANs implement some sort of printer spooling feature, meaning that individual users' printer output is actually written to disk by the network OS, then sent to the assigned network printer in turn. This usually has the side benefit of speeding up programs that normally spend a great deal of time waiting for what is, to a computer, an unusually slow printer. The printer spooling arrangements vary, but usually there is some method of changing the order in which jobs are printed and of changing the printer on which they are physically printed.

Large hard disks (up to 100 megabytes) are also popular peripherals, but different types of LANs support different maximum capacities on a single device. To further confuse the issue, some LANs and some multiuser application software designed for LAN use allow more than one physical disk to be considered one logical disk; this could result in one drive (appearing to the user as, say G:) having a capacity of over 200 megabytes (i.e., 2 units of 100 + megs each.)

When considering super economy sized hard disks, remember that many, if not most, application programs limit their file sizes to the largest size permitted by the operating system for which they are designed. For an IBM PC application, a maximum file size of 32 megabytes is common regardless of the actual size of the storage device in use. Ask.

Remember, too, that software must be designed for multiuser use; putting regular software on a common hard disk will not make it usable by several people at one time. See the section on Multiuser LAN Software below.

Some LANs have provision for a communications server that controls access to one or several modems, allowing 20 or 30 network users, each of whom has an occasional need for dial out access to some distant computer, to share a few modems. Modems are inexpensive, at least the slower ones, so this might not be the major cost saving that printer sharing is, however.

Other shareable peripherals, and the required supporting software, are under development by many companies.

LAN Software

The operating system software that, working in conjunction with the network hardware, allows a user access to the LAN, is generally available from either of two sources:

The network hardware vendor

A network software vendor

All the LAN hardware vendors have operating systems (OS) products used with their hardware products, and many have, in addition to workstation hardware and OS products, file server hardware and OS products. There are a great number of different vendors in this area. Some vendors have more than one type of LAN available, and others subscribing to one or the other standards.

In addition, there are several companies who have developed LAN OS products that work on other companies' hardware; one is Novell, Inc., whose

NetWare network OS products are available for use with most LAN hardware vendors' products.

There are also several software—only LAN products available, most of them using the serial communications ports already built in to most computers; this is a low cost approach, but the speed of communications over serial ports is limited. This could be a viable approach, however, for LANs whose major task is printer sharing, since the serial port speeds are much faster than most printers. One such product is LAN-Link, by The Software Link, Dunwoody, GA.

Multiuser LAN Software

To function in a multiuser environment, software must have been designed for the task to which it is put; merely putting your single user order entry system on your LAN and giving 11 people access to it will not make it a multiuser system. LAN vendors are infamous for blurring this distinction, using phrases like record locking and file locking. The facts are that the LAN cannot know what the programs are up to unless the programs tell the LAN, and single user programs are not designed to tell. Let us, then, discuss some multiuser concepts:

MULTIUSER: *Hardware*. A system that several people can use at the same time. The hardware use of the term does not indicate whether those several people can do the same thing at the same time, or not. Some minicomputers, for instance, are multiuser but the software available for them keeps each user's data in a separate file; the files must be combined in a separate operation.
Software. Programs that control each individual user's access to the data, under application program control. Usually, each user's program checks out part of the data, and during the time the data is checked out other users have no access to it. See Locking, below.

MULTITASKING: *Hardware*. Implies that the central processing unit (CPU) can divide its attention among several jobs, either for one user (single-user-multitasking or SUMT) or for several users (multiuser-multitasking or MUMT).

Software. Refers to an OS or LAN OS product that controls the CPU in its multitasking scheme.

Multitasking generally does not imply any sort of data sharing or locking arrangement.

LOCKING: *Software*. Indicates that the OS or the application controls access to data so that changes to the data may be made in an orderly fashion, i.e. user A does not change the record user B is changing without user B being aware of user A's change.

Locking is usually implemented on one of three levels: file locking, page locking, or record locking.

FILE LOCKING: Usually provided by the LAN OS, File locking assures integrity of files on multiuser systems by assuring that only one user has access to a file at a time. From the moment user A begins work on a file, until the software closes it (and some older software doesn't close its files), no other user can access any part of the file. Quite safe, but very inconvenient; might as well go back to manila folders. If at this point might use multitasking.

PAGE LOCKING: Provided by the application program (i.e. general ledger) via the LAN OS, page locking dedicates part of a file to one user at a time, allowing other users access to other parts of the same file when using the same or other software that subscribes to the same locking scheme. The LAN OS usually locks the file for other users who are not using the same page locking scheme. Page locking is vastly superior to file locking, but locks up larger pieces of files than does record locking; it is widely used because it is simpler to implement than true record locking, yet is just as effective in many situations.

RECORD LOCKING: Also provided by the application program (i.e. general ledger) via the LAN OS, record locking dedicates only the actual record(s) in use by each user at a particular time, allowing other users access to all other parts of the same file. The usual access method restrictions apply, just as in page locking. The LAN OS usually locks the file for other users who are not using the same locking scheme.

15

PROTECTING THE DATA

OVERVIEW

There is no better way to increase your productivity than by not losing your data. It sounds ridiculous, but it is true. Even the most experienced programmers and software users lose data. A microcomputer is fast, but it is an electronically based machine. The way the machine stores information makes that information very vulnerable to being wiped out, zapped, erased, written over, deleted, or just plain lost. This can happen in many different ways. Information can be stored on diskettes, cartridges, a hard disk, or some other media. Each type of storage media provides different risks. However, they all can have similar problems.

The loss of data is a common occurrence, whether through physical destruction or incorrect input into a valid data base by unknowledgeable or unauthorized personnel. The potential for loss becomes greater as micros become more powerful and are used by smaller companies with less trained personnel. Since hard-disks store more information than floppy diskettes, there is an even greater need for protection against the loss of data. Each of these causes of lost data are described in this chapter with suggestions for preventing the actual loss. Table 15–1 indicates some examples, causes, and possible solutions for protection.

One main way of protection against the physical loss of data is to keep current copies of the data readily available so that any lost data can be quickly

TABLE 15–1 Examples, Causes, and Protection of Data

Causes of Loss of Data	Possible Solutions
1. Physical loss of data	1. Procedures—backup, add-on equipment, security
2. Input errors	2. Control totals and security
3. Unauthorized access	3. Procedures—security, passwords
4. Misfiling data	4. Procedures—data library, backup

restored. A back up procedure that uses correct labeling and is performed often is one of the best means of protection available.

Also, certain types of equipment, such as a surge protector, provide another means of protecting your data against physical loss. However, procedures are a necessity. Without established procedures the additional equipment offers very little protection. Established procedures that control the computer environment are an essential ingredient to ensure accurate and timely use of previously entered data. Productivity is greatly reduced if there is continuing concern for the integrity or vulnerability of the data. The procedures do not have to be complex or time consuming if properly planned and implemented. Any additional cost is usually immaterial when compared to the potential benefits.

Not all of the steps that are suggested have to be taken. However, consideration should be given to them and to any others that are appropriate to the specific application being used. The company's management should make a decision as to which procedures are appropriate for their company.

In addition to procedural and hardware solutions, data protection should also include security to prevent input errors and protect confidentiality. Unauthorized persons with access to the data are risks because of inadvertent errors as well as confidentiality considerations. They and others could enter incorrect information or change files, models, and transactions in areas where detecting the change could be difficult. Inadvertent errors being made into valid data are a large enough risk without the additional concern of having unauthorized persons entering data. Unauthorized persons include untrained personnel who do not know how to enter the information correctly. To recover from such a problem can be very difficult, especially when large amounts of information are being manipulated or stored. For example, recovery would be difficult with spreadsheets that operate on a 512K micro or with an accounting file stored on the common 10M hard disk. Even though we are talking about micros, the amount of data being dealt with still can be very large.

Micros are not the game or hobbyist machines that they once were. With the development of the 640K or larger internal memories, 16 and 32 bit technology, multiuser, telecommunications, and 30M disk drives being connected to micros, it is a problem in the micro software world that they are not considered seriously enough. With mainframe access micros have enormous storage and operating capabilities.

Security is important in protecting information from being entered by the wrong people and in protecting it from being destroyed or changed in error, thereby significantly affecting the productive use of the information. For example, there should only be a few people with the appropriate access to enter invoices or payments. This could be accomplished by limiting the number of people who are trained and authorized to do those two functions. A person can be authorized to use one computer, but not another. Using this technique allows wide access to the computers while protecting the integrity of the information.

Even if the data is physically protected and secured, misfiling can make the information difficult to locate on a timely basis, which affects its availability to you just as if it were permanently lost. Using spreadsheets has shown many classical examples of misfiled information. Before you realize it, you can end up with a stack of diskettes with all kinds of file names you cannot find. Where was that model for the 1990's forecast? Where was the return on investment analysis for the new store you did a month ago? Filing diskettes with each one holding many workpapers is even harder. Each workpaper may be a file or a part of several files. A few months from now or even a few days from now, a file named Balance Sheet 1 looks just like a file named Balance Sheet 2. It is similar to the person who can work with stacks of papers on a desk and always know exactly where in the pile a specific piece of information is located. However, most of us need some form of organization to be able to find things.

PROBLEM PREVENTION

Just as in other areas, success in dealing with microcomputers frequently depends on some of the simplest things. For example, a NASA space rocket has significant problems because of something as small as a nut or a screw. Similarly, problems with a microcomputer can be caused by something outside of the machine and its basic application software. The problems could be caused by items that are generally taken for granted. For example, a forgotten power cord could cause the loss of a major sale because the microcomputer cannot be turned on without it. Fortunately for the user at the convention, the local electrical store was still open.

Hardware add-ons, software add-ons, and checklists can prevent serious problems from occurring. In this section there are some recommendations that can aid in preventing problems, such as a checklist so a power cord will not be forgotten. Each list, checklist, and matrix can be tailored to the specific situation and user needs. Checklists 15-1 and 15-2 are examples for use as defined control checklists.

Example	Recommendation	Description
1.	Checklist for moving equipment	Example of a checklist made before moving a microcomputer. Even with portable micros, there are items that need to be brought along.
2.	Supplies list	In using micros certain supplies should be kept on hand. An example of a list is shown. For example, to be without a formatted diskette when all the others are full is a problem.
3.	Input device matrix	Various devices are available for entering information into a micro. The majority are simple. However, choosing the right one in the right situation could significantly affect productivity.
4.	More power to your computer	List of hardware computer items that aid in usage and increase productivity.

Checklist 15–1

Steps in Moving Microcomputer

A. Lock computer head
B. Pack or bring the following:

1. Hardware

    Microcomputer

    Monitor

    Keyboard

    Letter quality printer

2. Detachable Cords and Cables

    Power supply cord

    Cable to printer

3. Diskettes Needed

    Operating disk

    Utility data disk

    Program data disks

        Electronic spreadsheet program

        Financial analysis disk

        Industry data disk

    Word processing program

        Special correspondence disk

    Inventory program

4. Supplies

    Printer paper

    Box of 10 blank diskettes

    Printer cartridge ribbon

5. Passwords

    Knowledge on current month's passwords. Manuals and Reference Materials

    Electronic spreadsheet quick reference guide

    Word processing reference card

CHECKLIST 15–2

Checklist of Microcomputer Supplies to be Kept on Hand

STORAGE MEDIA

1. Blank Diskettes (high quality). Diskettes can and do fail. They do not format or they stop working. All are vulnerable to abuse and wear and tear. Even cartridge back up tapes are susceptible.

2. Formatted diskettes. Certain quantity of diskettes that are prepared to receive information should be available. Especially since they are not formatted when purchased.

3. Labels for diskettes

4. Write protect tabs for diskettes

DISKETTE STORAGE

5. Holder (box, file, etc.) for diskettes

PRINTER

6. Letter Paper. Single Sheets or Continuous Feed

7. Wide Computer Paper Continuous Feed

8. Printer Cartridge Ribbons

9. Disk Drive Cleaner

OTHER SUPPLIES

10. Felt Tip Pens to Write on Diskette Labels

11. Wide Hardcover Computer Binders for Printouts

Table 15–2 provides an example of a useful matrix that could be used to determine input devices for company application. A similar matrix can be developed for output options.

TABLE 15–2 Matrix of Microcomputer Input Devices to Specific Company Application

Application	Keyboard	Bar Code Scanner	Modem	Writing Pad	Word Scanner	Mouse	Touch Screen	Coxial Cable	Video Disk
1. Normal number input	X	X							
2. Heavy word proc input from typed matter					X				
3. External databases			X						
4. Transfer of internal company information inside building							X		
5. Written sales orders direct from sales personnel			X	X					
6. Charts, graphs and similar types of presentations				X		X			
7. Input of information by computer novices						X	X		
8. Picture representations									X

PROTECTION OF DATA

An overview

Physical loss of data

Input errors

Misfiling data

Backup

Figures 15–1 and 15–2 discuss the most important protection methods. Table 15–3 shows major areas causing physical loss and protection against each.

1. Backup
2. Backup
3. Backup

FIGURE 15–1 Three Must Rules

CUT OUT

PUT ON COMPUTER

DID YOU DO YOUR
BACKUP TODAY?

FIGURE 15–2

PHYSICAL LOSS OF DATA

The computer and its storage media are electronic. Therefore, they are vulnerable to static electricity, power supply changes, and many other electrically induced problems. Care should be taken in storing, using, and moving the media. Also, theft or computer crime is a whole risk in itself.

In addition, care should be taken with the hardware. One problem is caused by the newer office buildings that are sealed so no windows can be opened. During the weekends when the ventilation system is shut off, the

TABLE 15–3 Four Major Areas that Cause Physical Loss of Software Data

Causes	Possible Protection
Power Related	
Power surges—changes in power	Backup, hardware add on Surge protector
Loss of power	Backup, Surge protector
Static	Surge Protector, Nonstatic rugs, Spray for rugs, Static mat under computer
Hardware Related	
Hardware problems, for example, disk drive out of alignment	Monthly maintenance contract, hardware checkup, backups
Temperature-high temperature can cause a microcomputer to stop working	Do not operate the microcomputer when the building cooling system is not working unless you have a separate cooling system.
Media Related—Diskettes	
Bending diskettes Laying on top of terminals Allowing them to be x-rayed Writing on diskettes with the wrong instrument	Backup, purchase quality diskettes, write on labels with felt tipped pens, be careful in handling diskettes, and do not allow any of the items on the left to occur
User Related	
Incorrect usage of utility routines and end of period processing wiping out data	There are many powerful utility commands that can be used. One is erase and another is format. Both will wipe out all data. Be very careful in using these types of commands. Their effect is permanent. Be sure to always do backups before doing this type of task. Many change the name of these utilities to another name so users can not use the format command. Only authorized people have access to the proper command. Put write protect tabs on disks that should not be changed.
Sabotage or destruction on purpose	External utilities lock out use of hard disk micros' passwords. Physical protection of micros through locked rooms or machine locking devices

rooms can get very hot. If an operator is working during one of these hot weekends, the computer can overheat and stop working. Then, the hardware has been damaged and whatever information the operator was working on could be lost.

Another problem can occur when a company moves into offices with plush pile rugs. The microcomputer is set on a table. One day the operator brushes along the carpet, touches the micro, and sends a static electrical charge through the computer, damaging the equipment and the media. Another potential problem occurs when a power line is cut and power goes out while the computer is on. The data being used at that time could be lost. Figure 15–3 indicates three other examples of losing data and some possible suggestions.

Message on screen, Nonsystem disk.
Tip: Load disk that has operating system. In using MS DOS each disk can have the operating system on it by formatting with /s command or format /s. Remember, the operating system must be loaded into the computer before the application program can be used.

You've just erased all the data on a valuable diskette.
Tip: Save the diskette and get a utility software program which has the function of regaining lost files. Often some files (perhaps all) can be reconstructed.

You've turned off the computer before saving your data to diskette.
Tip: Take an aspirin and be ready to stay late to redo your work.
SAVE TO DISKETTE OFTEN.

FIGURE 15–3 Tips on What To Do after You Did It Wrong

The aforementioned problems seem to arise from simple causes, many affecting even a television. Although micros are called high tech tools, some basic electrical problems still exist.

INPUT ERRORS

Errors can be entered into the computer as easily as in a manual system. The computer cannot tell if an entry should be $2,000 or $200. Many programs will perform basic editing, such as not allowing letters to be placed where numbers belong or checking that the debits and credits of an entry balance. The rest is up to you. Accounting packages by their nature have more specific input controls than DBMS programs and electronic spreadsheets. A general ledger knows it is supposed to act as a general ledger. However, a data base manager is much more flexible. Controls ouside the computer must exist.

COMPUTER THEFT

Computer theft or improper access should be a concern. Computer security can stop your insecurity.

Usually, a company wants to protect certain information, such as payroll, company financial information, and customer records, from being available to all personnel, to protect confidentiality and privacy. In addition, letters in a word processor, models in an electronic spreadsheet, and customer lists in a list manager package may need to be kept confidential, just as they would be in paper form. Therefore, for confidentiality reasons, whether on diskette or on paper, the same care must be taken in assuring that confidentiality. Also, security methods can stop unauthorized use to prevent problems being entered into the data. Just as all company personnel should not drive the company truck, they should not all operate the company microcomputer. Although the utilization of micros should be encouraged as much as possible, these problems do have to be considered. One possible solution is to allocate certain computers for all personnel to use and to maintain control over separate computers that are critical to the operations or record keeping task.

The big breakthrough of the microcomputer is its ability to provide computer power to all. However, the micro has to be controlled just as any other resource in the company.

Besides the data itself, the actual coding for the software's programs may be accessible to the user. The purchaser of the software should know this before using the software. If this is applicable, then security for the programming code in the software has to be considered. A change to the program could cause extensive problems throughout a company's operations. The software is easier to maintain and support with access to the programs; however, there must be security measures in place to protect against unauthorized or unknown changes to the programs.

FOUR BASIC SECURITY METHODS TO USE

1. Physical security relating to hardware

Limit access to microcomputer.

Lock micro in separate room.

Install locking unit to keyboard where a physical key must be used before the keyboard will work.

2. Passwords

   Use passwords to limit the number of persons with the ability to start up a program to access a particular routine.

   Use passwords to limit access capabilities to specific submenus. For example, the password could be set up to allow only query capabilities, to enter only certain transactions without the capability of updating the master files, or setting up new ones.

3. Physical security relating to the storage media

   Store the media in a specific place

   Lock up the media after use.

   Use the appropriate procedure for making the diskettes so that they cannot be copied or have files written on them.

4. Security relating to software

   Restrict computers so that specific software functions are done on specific computers.

   Protect actual software programs from having changes made to them by compiling (making them compressed and unreadable, for the most part) the programs in the software package.

   Restrict changes to the code. A change could create a miscalculation later or a change in one part of the program could affect its operation in another part. Program changes should be made only in a controlled environment.

   Add a locking disk technology to software diskette.

Even though you operate a hard-disk computer, put all spreadsheets and word processing files on diskettes that can be physically locked up. If the software does allow changes made to the programs by the user, there should be definite security measures established to control the changes being made. Many times the software may have to be modified to address a specific user demand. This should be done under the strictest control, as if it were a new software package including testing and running dual systems before using the new code.

Computer software codes should only be modified if allowed by the vendor license agreement. All users must be careful of improper copying of software and nonallowable modification and use. A company computer security policy should be established within the standard company policies to cover this.

MISFILING DATA

Those little diskettes—how do you find anything on them? A data library can be very useful for locating information that is on a diskette. After using a microcomputer for a time many diskettes are accumulated. Even with a hard disk, files have to be named and diskettes or tapes are accumulated through using them to make backups. It is easy to forget the purpose, utilization, and date of a particular file. Office productivity software packages hold the greatest danger for misfiling—where spreadsheets, word processing letters, and lists proliferate. Data files are named by a user by an alpha numeric code. If 20 diskettes with 10 files each are being maintained, that is 200 files. Even in accounting, back up diskettes and cartridges can be dated or labeled incorrectly. This is especially true if a company is using more than one software package such as accounts receivable, accounts payable, and general ledger.

Steps should be taken to store, label, and categorize the information properly. Again, it is not obvious by looking at a diskette or hard disk what information is on them. Therefore, some type of library system should be put in place. Any library system must have two aspects:

1. A naming convention established
2. A physical storage arrangement (for disks and tapes)

In a library for books there is a code found on the bottom of the book to indicate where the book belongs in the library. Then the book is physically stored that way. This same technique can be used with a data library for storage media. Establish a coding system for identifying diskettes and the files that are on them. Table 15–4 shows an example of a library system.

A file-naming structure and a data library should be established to control

TABLE 15–4 Library Summary

Applications	Labels on Diskettes	Data Files	What It Starts With
Electronic Spreadsheet	Budget	BUD	Budget—for 1988, 1989, and each quarter
	Projections	PROJ	Projections for 1990 and 1991
	Sales	SALEAN	Sales analysis for each month, quarter, and year-to-date 1987. Analysis by product, sales region, and store. Includes format for sales analysis report.
Word Processing	Letters August 87	LTA87	Letters on general correspondence August, 1987
	Memos to employees	MEMOEMP	Memos to employees for 1987
	Reports	REP	Formats for reports to management and for letters
Accounts Receivable	A/R Transactions Jan 10—Oct 87	Monthly financial transactions January 1987 to October 1987	
	Program diskettes	Accounts receivable program diskette	
	Backup program	Backup program diskette	
	1986 data	Transactions for year-end December 31, 1986	

the media. This can be as simple or as sophisticated as desired, based on the usage of the micro. In establishing appropriate procedures consider

Amount of information

Speed with which the information has to be recalled

Specific company situation

There are certain software and media conventions that can help in this area. Some computers have automatic time clocks and most allow the date to be entered. This is useful because some accounting software allows an entire year of transactions to be displayed instead of only a month. This is important because only one file in a general ledger needs to be kept for all of the transactions in an account such as cash. Otherwise, you need to refer to 12 separate printouts or diskettes to follow a year's transactions. Even the use of a hard disk does not solve this situation automatically. Analyzing customer accounts could become very difficult if the history files are scattered over several diskettes. The following steps are suggestions for setting up a data library.

STEPS THAT AID IN CREATING A LIBRARY

1. Establish coding or naming routine. Date and enter code or name on all labels on all diskettes.
2. Establish a naming convention for the files, such as spreadsheet models or letters on a word processor. Examples: BALSHQ486 could be used to mean balance sheet for the fourth quarter of 1986 and LBANKA could be used to mean a letter written to the bank in August. The naming convention needs to be altered based on the frequency of the letters.
3. Enter the current date when the computer is first turned on. Many micros will enter a date next to the file name if the date is entered when the computer is first turned on. Many users do not take the time to enter the current date when first turning on the computer.
4. Establish a predefined physical arrangement for the diskettes or cartridges. Don't just toss them in the most convenient box or drawer.
5. Label all diskettes. Be sure to use a felt tip pen.
6. Print the file names periodically and indicate what they are. This is useful

when using office productivity software as well as accounting software. Use the DIR utility (if using MS DOS) that comes with your computer's operating system. When you turn on the computer a system prompt appears (A:). At this point, type DIR. Frequently, the computer keyboard has a print screen key. Use this key to print the file names. If your computer does not have a print screen key, write down the list of file names.

The library should be summarized from time to time to show what is available. This becomes more critical in larger situations such as multiuser and networking systems. The integrity of the files and what is available is more important. Various methods can be used to control a library varying from simple to very formal procedures. The larger the organization and the need for coordination, the more important steps like these become.

STEPS THAT CAN BE TAKEN TO SUMMARIZE A LIBRARY

1. Simple—Type list of diskettes and summary of what each contains.
2. More formal—Maintain card catalog just like a library would of three-by-five cards listing each diskette.
3. Formal—Use a small data base manager or list manager to organize diskettes and machine files into logical file arrangement. Method is:
   a. One file in data base can list the programs available.
   b. Second file can list the data diskettes available.
   c. Information in both files can be sorted by preestablished methods using keys. Keys or codes for sorting will designate for data files:

      Type of software program to which data is connected.

      Data diskettes available.

      Authorization codes connected to each file.

      Authorization code is equal to passwords and indicate who has access authority to a specific diskette and its files.

BACKUP

Using backups is an excellent procedure to recover from loss whether it is through physical loss, input errors, or misfiling of data. This cannot be overemphasized because doing the backup is easy to forget. When dealing with a job's daily pressures and activities, doing backups can be the hardest thing to remember.

Most office productivity products and many accounting products do not require automatic backup. In addition, frequently there is no mention in the software manual about making backups because the assumption is made that the user knows to do them.

The use of a hard disk can compound this problem rather than resolve it. The amount of data stored is larger; therefore, copying the data takes longer. If diskettes are used to back up a hard disk, a volume of diskettes is created. There are tape backup machines and backup utilities that make this process much quicker.

STEPS IN BACKUP PROCEDURES

1. Written documents	Save computer printouts and original documents
2. Copy files on diskette	Backup files (normally relevant to office productivity software on the same diskette with different file name)
3. Copy diskettc	Copy master diskette to another one and store separately
4. Copy diskette and store	Copy master diskette to another one and store outside the building

Backup procedures include:

1. Written documents. The documents created by the computer and those already outside the computer create an automatic backup for much of the information on the computer storage media. Therefore:

   Store original documents in a logical order (such as cash receipts reports and hand written sales orders). Store original documents in a place where they can be located again, such as file drawers or microfilm original documents.

Print reports, even though they are not required, such as transaction reports in accounting software. These reports are useful as audit trails. Store printouts in a logical manner. They can be stored in some type of binder that will protect them.

2. Copy files on diskette. In office productivity software, spreadsheets and letters are assigned names given by the user.
   a. Give a file another name and save it on the same diskette.
   b. Use common designation for a backup name.

      Example: Use B in front of all file names.

Spreadsheet:	Original-BUD88
	Backup-BBUD88
Word processing:	Original-MANREP
	Backup-BMANREP

   c. Determine if software automatically creates a backup on the same diskette. Some packages create a backup file by changing the file name extension (the three letters after the assigned name).
   d. Copy a file on the same diskette with a different name. It is a good idea to put the file name in the first block of the spreadsheet.
3. Copy diskette to another and store this backup copy.
   a. Backup procedures. Set up a procedure for backing up to other diskettes.
   b. Sign-off log. One way to be sure backups are being prepared is to maintain a routine sign off log. When the copy is made, the operator would then sign the sign off log. Table 15–5 is an example of a sign off log.
   c. Rotating backup procedure. A way to make sure there are always current backups is to use a rotating procedure. For example, there could be a procedure to ensure that there are always two backups—one that is a week old and one that is two weeks old. By using this method, if one backup is lost, there is another available. This procedure can eliminate the possibility of having to reenter all of the data being used in the system. No more than two weeks worth of data would have to be reentered. These backups should always be kept current to prevent any more reentry than is absolutely necessary.

TABLE 15–5 Quarterly Backup Control Form Sign-Off Log

				Period covered: Third quarter	
Date Week Ending	Programs			Date File Listing Produced	Date Taken Off Site
	Spreadsheets	*G/L*	*A/R*		
10/5	*LS	*AB	*AB		
10/12	LS	AB	AB		10/8
10/19	LS	AB	AB		
10/26	LS	AB	AB	10/28	
11/2	LS	AB	AB		
11/9	LS	AB	AB		
11/16	LS	AB	AB		
11/23	LS	AB	AB	11/23	
11/30	LS	AB	AB		
12/7	LS	AB	AB		
12/14	LS	AB	AB		
12/21	LS	AB	AB		
12/28	LS	AB	AB	12/28	
12/31	LS	AB	AB		

*Backup initials

A good way to keep up with rotating backups is to use color coded diskette labels or different color diskettes. Also, the backups should always be dated as to when they were prepared. When the current diskette goes bad, frequently a user will put the backup in the computer and start using it, only to find out that the computer's disk drive is so bad that the backup diskette has been eaten. The rotating backup procedure offers protection against this type of problem. When storing disks in safes remember they are plastic media. A fire can still destroy them depending on the safe.

d. Keep data only on diskettes. Maintain only programs on hard disk. This method does defeat some of the advantages of using a hard disk. However, if there are several people using the same micro, it can be very useful for each person to keep their individual data on separate diskettes. Each week do a directory of the hard disk to be sure there are not data files on it. This method has an added security advantage—only the person who needs access to the data has it, because the data is being physically stored by the appropriate individual. This approach is more appropriate if using office productivity packages rather than accounting applications. In accounting, the data normally needs to be on the hard disk for quick access capabilities.

e. End of period processing. At the end of a period (month, year) many accounting software packages automatically produce a backup copy. The procedure is

   Run end of period processing.

   The current transactions are closed on another diskette and become history; data and balances are updated.

   The old diskette used as an original becomes a backup.

   A new diskette becomes the current period's diskette.

4. Off site Storage. Besides maintaining copies of data in the office, a copy should be stored off the premises. It is very important to make a copy to keep off site right after first installing the system, because this copy would contain the company parameters and master file information. Even after building basic models and letter files an off site copy should be maintained. Special vault facilities exist for this kind of storage. In a small company, taking it home (as long as it does not effect control) is off site storage. Of course storage at home creates other risks. A preassigned formal location is best. This procedure is useful no matter what storage media is used.

16

RESOURCES AVAILABLE TO THE LONELY USER

TRAINING

Training is a very necessary part of being able to obtain a return on the microcomputer software and hardware investment. There are a number of sources for training.

HANDS-ON COURSES

Hands-on courses are very important.

Courses are available from many places including:

National Association of Accountants

American Institute of CPAs

State CPA chapters

Schools

Local training centers

INTERACTIVE COMPUTERIZED TRAINING

An important training tool is interactive video disk training. This is performed by using a laser disk player and an interactive video unit. You view the course like a television show, however one that you can interact with by answering questions and moving to specific topics that you want to cover based on menu selection. One company providing such an offering is Comsell, Inc. in Atlanta, Ga.

Hands-on courses are very important. However interactive video disk can be used for retraining.

These courses are valuable as stand-alone or as a supplement to another course. The course can also allow the user to be within the training program and then switch over to practice the exercise in the actual software.

OTHERS

Other forms are available, such as tutorials from vendors, exercise books, and many less structured training vehicles.

DICTIONARIES OF COMPUTER TERMS

1. *Dictionary of Information Technology*
   Dennis Longley and Michael Shain
   John Wiley & Sons, New York, NY, 1982
   Provides detail descriptions of many different terms.
2. *Webster's New World Compact Dictionary of Computer Terms*
   Compiled by Laura Darey and Louise Boston
   Simon and Schuster, New York, NY, 1983
   Small pocket size dictionary.
3. *Dictionary of Computers, Data Processing, and Telecommunications*
   Jerry Martin Rosenberg
   John Wiley & Sons, New York, NY, 1984
   Lists all three types of definitions in one book. For technical people and novices.
4. *The Illustrated Computer Dictionary*
   Bantam Books
   From the editors of Consumer Guide
   Simple dictionary of computer terms using illustrations.
5. *A Dictionary of Computer Words*
   Robert Bly
   Dell
   Easy terminology of some basic computer terms
6. Manuals with specific software packages.
   Many software packages include a glossary.

An example is the Symphony package from Lotus Development Corporation. A separate glossary book comes with the software package.

PUBLICATIONS THAT KEEP YOU UP-TO-DATE

Professional Associations

1. Books in Wiley/Ronald-National Association of Accountants Professional Book Series
2. *Journal of Accountancy*
   Published monthly by
   American Institute of Certified Public Accountants
   1211 Avenue of the Americas
   New York, NY 10036
3. *Management Accounting*
   Published monthly by
   The National Association of Accountants
   10 Paragon Drive
   Montvalc, NJ 07645
4. Newsletters from NAA and other professional associations
5. Practice aids, special reports, and other reports
   From the American Institute of Certified Public Accountants
6. Other Professional and Trade magazines
   For specific industry software
   (vertical market software)

Computer Magazines

Magazines oriented toward the microcomputer provide up-to-date information to users and practical tips in using current technology. Even the advertisements in these magazines are a valuable source of current computer information. Some of these magazines follow. They can be subscribed to or found in book stores, computer retail stores, or local libraries.

1. *Byte*
   Published monthly by

McGraw-Hill, Inc.
One Phoenix Mill Lane
Peterborough, NH 03458

2. *Lotus—Computing for Managers and Professionals*. Has very specific and practical tips on how to use Lotus products.
Published monthly by
Lotus Publishing Corporation
55 Cambridge Parkway
Cambridge, MA 02142

3. *PC Magazine*
Published biweekly by
Ziff-Davis Publishing Co.
One Park Avenue
New York, NY 10016

4. *PC World*
Published monthly by
PCW Communications, Inc.
501 Second Street
San Francisco, CA 94107

5. *Personal Computing*
Published monthly by
Hayden Publishing Company, Inc.
10 Mulholland Drive
Hasbrouck Heights, NJ 07604
Many of these and other magazines provide analysis and comparison of popular microsoftware and technology.

Sources for Listings of Microsoftware

1. *Data Sources*
Ziff-Davis Publishing Company
Printed quarterly
Two large volumes with detail listings by software category with description of software and vendor

2. *Software Digest*, Inc.
An independent monthly rating newsletter. No advertisements shown
Printed monthly

3. Datapro Research Corporation
   Large volumes showing directory of software

4 AICPA Computer Technical Information
   Provided by the Microcomputer Services Division
   Provides to AICPA members information about hardware and software and telephone support

5. *Addison-Wesley Book of IBM Software 1984*
   Robert P. Wells, Ph.D., Sandra Rochowansky, and Michael Mellin, Ph.D.

6. *OMNI Complete Catalog of Computer Software*
   Collier Books
   Edited by Owen Davies

Review of Software Sources

1. Various computer magazines

2. *Software Digest*, Inc.
   Ratings newsletter

Where to Look for Personal Help

The following does not indicate that one firm or type of firm is better than the other.

1. CPA Firms

   Big eight CPA firms have worked with and reviewed the most popular microsoftware.

   Instead of a request for proposal (RFP), they have allocated time and resources to review microsoftware so cost effective advice can be given. An RFP concentrates on a single installation. Just as microsoftware was developed on a standard basis rather than customized, the advice has been developed in the same way. It is difficult to charge large fees for one hundred dollar software.

   Many CPA firms have separate centralized microsoftware departments responsible for controlling this process. Some have small business consulting departments that provide aid or business advice that would include using microcomputer technology.

National and international second tier firms These also are involved in microsoftware as many deal extensively with small businesses. Some have central microcomputer consulting departments and have done the same as the big eight.

Regional and local firms

Most maintain some expertise in microcomputers unless they define their practice to income tax or a very specific level of service. Some use the resources of a CPA association or other larger CPA firms to provide assistance on microcomputers. The microcomputer area is changing so rapidly that a commitment must be made to service this area.

2. Consultants

   Computer consulting firms
   General management consultants
   Internal company consultants

3. Some industry associations

   Sell software

   Endorse software

   Recommend software

   Computer shows

   Trade shows

   Computer dealer shows
   held at Atlanta, GA—Spring
   Las Vegas, Nevada—Fall

   NAA Seminars

   AICPA seminars

   State CPA chapter computer seminars

   CPAs can turn to the American Institute of CPAs (AICPA) technical information department in New York

   Training seminars—AICPA, state chapters, NAA offer seminars

4. Facility coordinators

   Many corporations have set up facility coordinators who coordinate utilization of microcomputer technology. They act as go-between for the users and the data processing departments.

5. Software vendors—Many vendors assist users before and after the sale.

6. Training centers—Local training centers provide specific classes.
7. Business computer dealers—computer stores specialize in business systems including maintaining complete training centers.
8. Local user groups

Some of the computer retail dealers throughout the country are:

Businessland
Computerland
Microage Computer Stores
Sears Business Systems Center

Common Types of Computer based training

Many other resources are available and should be sought out by the user.

LIST OF SPREADSHEETS

INDEX